D1112122

Kristi Ling's willingness to share her story and be a living example of what science is telling us—that we can train ourselves to be happy—shows us all that happiness is always available if we're willing to deliberately *do* it rather than just wait around for it.

—*Arielle Ford, author of* Turn Your Mate into Your Soulmate

As a firm believer in pro-active participation in every aspect of our lives, I love the way Kristi Ling has extended this philosophy to our pursuit of happiness. It's all about personal responsibility, greater awareness, and taking positive action. *Operation Happiness* is the perfect road map!

—*Susan Wilking Horan, wellness advocate and bestselling author of* The Single Source Cancer Course

Never has a book like *Operation Happiness* been more relevant! At a time when we're searching for the next "like," or external validation, Kristi Ling teaches us that happiness is a skill and ultimately our responsibility to learn and master.

—*Corey Jenkins, inspirational speaker and host of the talk show* Life with Awareness

OPERATION HAPPINESS

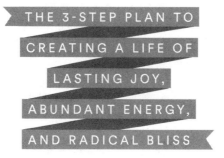

THE 3-STEP PLAN TO
CREATING A LIFE OF
LASTING JOY,
ABUNDANT ENERGY,
AND RADICAL BLISS

KRISTI LING

RODALE.

RODALE
wellness

Live happy. Be healthy. Get inspired.

Sign up today to get exclusive access to our authors, exclusive bonuses,
and the most authoritative, useful, and cutting-edge information on health,
wellness, fitness, and living your life to the fullest.

Visit us online at RodaleWellness.com
Join us at RodaleWellness.com/Join

Rodale books may be purchased for business or promotional use or for
special sales. For information, please write to:
Special Markets Department, Rodale Inc., 733 Third Avenue,
New York, NY 10017

Printed in the United States of America
Rodale Inc. makes every effort to use acid-free ⊗, recycled paper ♻.

Book design by Christina Gaugler

Library of Congress Cataloging-in-Publication Data is on file with the publisher.

ISBN 978–1–62336–594–3   hardcover

Distributed to the trade by Macmillan

2   4   6   8   10   9   7   5   3   1   hardcover

🌱 RODALE.

Follow us @RodaleBooks on

We inspire and enable people to improve their lives and the world around them.
rodalewellness.com

For my friends and family.
And for anyone who has ever felt like they've been wandering
the forest of life without a field guide for happiness.

ACKNOWLEDGMENTS

There are so many incredible people who have helped, supported, and inspired me in my journey and in the creation of this book. First, I would like to thank all four of my parents. You have all taught me so much more than you know. Mom, thank you for being my rock and for your love, honesty, strength, and grace. Dad, thank you for inspiring me with your entrepreneurial spirit. Keith (my second dad), I love and appreciate you so much. Jennifer, thank you for your joyful energy and for being a wonderful partner to my dad. Scott, Loren, Stacey, and Dana, I could not be a more fortunate sister. Thank you to my whole, big, wonderfully complex family—nieces, nephews, aunts, uncles, in-laws, and long lost (and newly discovered) family members. I love you all.

I would like to extend tremendous gratitude and appreciation to my literary agent Bill Gladstone. Thank you for believing in me and for guiding me to believe in myself even more. A huge thanks to my gifted editors Lora Sickora and Jennifer Levesque. Your support, brilliant suggestions, and guidance have been invaluable. Enormous thanks to Aly Mostel, Evan Klonsky, Alyse Diamond, Aaron Pattap, Chris Gaugler, and the entire team at Rodale. I'm honored to work with such a wonderful, mission-driven company that does so much to inspire people, improve lives, and help create a better world.

Thank you to friends, teachers, and mentors who were especially supportive with this book: T.R. Garland, Peggy McColl, Amateo Ra, Craig and Eddie Sanders, John Peterson, Jen Svejda, Maddy Bowman, Emmanuel Dagher, and Wendy L. Yost. And, thank you Mabel Katz for your Ho'oponopono guidance.

Endless thanks from my whole heart to dear ones who have offered endless support, inspiration, and brilliant insight: Richie

Jacquez and family; Mark Fleischer; Susan Wilking Horan; Betty Boop and the Fleischer Studios team; Linda Joy; Amy Prenner; Steve Truitt; Michael Goodman; Dylan Vigil; Kenn Henman; Kathy Buckley; Jennifer Currier; Betsy Johnson; Leslie Kaz; Leslie and Brad Story; Julie Andersen and the gang; Nick Ramirez; Benjamin Hisoler; the Bowman family; John Mulhall; Matt Orr; Sam Lucas and Clayton Yeung; Brittain Alexander; Denise Ridlon; Cory Sadler; and, of course, Robert. And, infinite gratitude to my many other friends and colleagues who have cheered me on (you know who you are).

A heartfelt thanks to my social media family, blog readers, and podcast listeners. I'm grateful every day to be connected and co-creating with such beautiful souls.

I would also like to acknowledge my beloved lifelong friends who left this world too soon: Rob Brown, Sharon Morgan, Mark Tortorici, and Blayne Alexander. Thank you for inspiring me, supporting me, and for all that I was so lucky to learn from you.

Finally, huge gratitude to all the trailblazing authors, teachers, and mentors who have inspired me with their wisdom and light in so many ways along my journey, including Thomas Leonard, Tony Robbins, Elizabeth Gilbert, Marianne Williamson, Guy Finley, Kris Carr, Tim Ferriss, Cheryl Richardson, Brendon Burchard, Oprah Winfrey, Neale Donald Walsch, and my third grade teacher Mr. Rhodes.

I'm so grateful for you all and for this amazing, mysterious, wild life. I am truly blessed.

CONTENTS

PART III—CREATE NEW HABITS + THIRTY DAYS OF INSIGHT, LOVE, AND LESSONS (A MONTHLONG DAYBOOK)

INTRODUCTION

Welcome to *Operation Happiness*! This book is a fired-up, life-shifting, crash course in happiness that will, among other things, create a powerful perspective shift to reveal an enormously overlooked, life-illuminating truth: *Happiness is a skill.* It's widely known as a choice, a feeling, a state of being, which is all true. But most important, it's an actual skill that can be learned, improved upon, and even mastered—just like playing a musical instrument or riding a bike. I believe this one powerful concept is the missing link that's been holding so many back from creating the amazing, dynamic lives they desire and deserve.

Crafting the happy, expansive, energetic life I'm living today wasn't an overnight journey for me, and it definitely wasn't easy. It took me nearly ten years, a ton of hard work, a few giant missteps, dedicated study, and being open to big lessons. Ten years may seem like a long time, but the truth is, after feeling broken and hitting rock bottom, I was trying to reverse and dissolve patterns that had been within me for more than thirty years. When you think of it that way, a decade doesn't seem so long. However, when I had the enormous realization eight years into that journey that happiness is actually a skill and started practicing it that way daily, my life changed. It was like I'd finally discovered my true nature and walked right into an entirely new, light-filled world. This magical approach is what this book is all about.

I've spent the last thirteen years immersed in the study and practice of happiness. I've read countless books; tried practical, scientific, and super "woo-woo" stuff; and been completely fascinated by it all. The first few years, it grew from my unrelenting desire to change my own life, but there came a point when I knew that all I was learning and discovering was so valuable, so life-changing, and so important, I had to share it with the world.

It's my intention to save you time, frustration, and grief by lighting the way for you to immediately step onto the extraordinary path that took me years to discover—the road to learning, practicing, and becoming damn good at the *skill* of happiness.

We should rethink well-meant phrases like "I'm so glad she's found happiness." Happy people don't find happiness like you'd find a penny on the ground; they make it happen with action. They cultivate and create it. They practice it daily. They relentlessly go after their dreams. They're not lucky; they're completely dedicated to their own joy and evolution.

> *"Happy people don't find happiness like you'd find a penny on the ground; they make it happen with action."*

That moment all those years ago when I made the firm, unwavering decision to use my own power to take charge of—and consciously create—my own happiness, my entire world changed in incredible ways. And you know what? I give myself a boatload of credit for it! Since you've picked up this book (I'm so thrilled you're here!), you are likely in that same place. Ready to take the wheel. To try something different. To stop settling for crumbs and go for major transformation. You are courageous, you are powerful, and you are a doer. You deserve all the credit in the world, too! Take a second to really breathe that in.

In this book, I've narrowed the road to happiness down to three multifaceted, powerful steps: *Change Your View, Make Over Your Mornings,* and *Create New Habits.* All are transforming and empowering when fully embraced.

Along our expedition together, I'll share some very personal stories with you, as well as a few confessions and major realizations. I'll offer my most surprising perspective shifts and biggest lightbulb moments from my own journey to happiness. We'll get into some specific how-tos, priority changes, and action steps to empower you to create a solid foundation for sustainable, radical happiness, energy, bliss, and success.

If you're open to letting go of old mind-sets and embracing empowering new ideas, ready to audaciously step out of your comfort zone, and willing to do the work it takes, then *Operation Happiness* is for you. The first step to being happy is being *willing* to be happy. And being willing means taking the action and doing the work, every single day. Many people are not happy simply because they're unwilling to make the effort.

IT'S TIME TO TAKE ACTION

The purpose of this book is not simply to get you thinking; it's to get you *doing*. Take action and make your very best life happen! I'll be pushing you—even kicking your butt a bit (with tons of love, of course)—because there's nothing I want more for you than the happiness you deserve. Your time is now. It won't be easy, but if you're willing to go all out, I will help you create sweeping, positive changes that will support you for the rest of your miraculous life.

I highly recommend you keep a journal or pad of paper on hand because you'll want to write down many things, including lists I'll be asking you to create. It's all about designing a brand-new, incredibly light-filled way of living full of purpose, activity, and, of course, happiness.

To help you along the way, I've divided the book into three parts—each dedicated to one of the three critical steps to learn and master the habit of happiness.

Part I—The Bigger Picture: Change Your View of Happiness

In this first section, I'll highlight a few stories from my own happiness journey and how I discovered, tested, and honed the powerful ideas shared in this book.

It's really about changing the way we look at happiness to think of it as a skill and as something that involves action we both consciously and physically create. Part of the skill of happiness is that we have to mindfully *do* it on a daily basis. There's science behind all this (your brain is your best friend), and we'll talk about that, too.

We'll dive into key happiness mind-sets and how to make them a prominent part of your life, creating more love and joy in your world in big ways. We'll explore completely new views of the events of your life, as well as some of the ones that may be going on right now. I'll show you how to create brand-new stories in your heart around circumstances in your life that will empower you instead of drain you.

We'll even get into some perspective shifts on happiness and strength during grief, loss, and difficult times, since everyone—even the happiest people—will experience these. The right happiness habits and mind-sets can illuminate the stars within the depths of darkness and make all the difference in healing and moving forward from setbacks in the best possible ways.

Part I will get you to a fantastic place to be totally open and ready for the rest of what's coming your way.

Part II—The Essential Shift: Make Over Your Mornings

"What's the first thing I should do if I want to be happier?" When people ask me this important question, I always have the same answer: *Make over your mornings*. The way you start your day creates the foundation for it—and your life. Changing your mornings to be more healthful, positive, and supportive is the single biggest shift you can make to create a happier life. This section is a potent, fun, how-to journey that will help you give your mornings (and days!) an energizing, empowering makeover.

I've been sharing this message passionately since 2009, when I discovered how the habits and mind-sets I was waking up with were so drastically shaping my days, and my entire life. Most people start the day rushing, stressing, and suffering from nutrition,

energy, and hydration deficits. I know I definitely used to. Permanently changing your mornings with subtle, powerful shifts and
positive, supportive new habits can literally change your whole life
and set the foundation for happier, more successful, incredibly
dynamic days—day after day.

Part II includes examples, actionable steps, worksheets, and tools
to help you dissolve draining morning habits that are blocking your
best life and create new, supportive morning routines and practices
that will propel you into brighter, more joyful days. It will cover key
changes for your morning routine and how to make over the spaces
where you spend your mornings to lift you up, speak to your soul,
and support your best life. We'll even go into an entirely new way to
view healthy eating and wellness that will connect your choices in
these areas to your deepest desires. It's all part of a holistic, empowered, spiritual approach to your mornings—and your life—that will
change the energy and joy levels of your world in big ways.

Part III—Create New Habits + Thirty Days of Insight, Love, and Lessons (A Monthlong Daybook)

Part III begins with a chapter about eleven key habits of the happiest people and how to begin adopting them. Our habits drastically
impact the way we experience life, and this section will cover some
great tips for dissolving the negative and creating the positive.

The end of this section is made up of a monthlong daybook
featuring thirty of my favorite essays and blog posts. This is meant
to offer you an immediate resource to begin creating the supportive
new habit of reading something uplifting each day. The insightful
little stories and lessons from my own life share perspective on
happiness, reaching for dreams, making transitions, creating success, overcoming fears, forgiveness, simplicity, kindness, and
growth through loss. I wanted this collection of stories to be like a
cool bonus at the end of the book. Bits of wisdom from my soul to
yours and for those you might wish to share them with.

Here's the deal: *I want this book to interrupt your life*—to shake up what you've been tolerating, accepting, and thinking in positive, monumental, change-creating ways. My goal is to help you construct big shifts in the way you've been thinking about and approaching not just happiness, but life, and to show you, step-by-step, exactly where and how to begin easily cultivating more lasting, sustainable joy, love, adventure, and peace.

Operation Happiness is not just intended to help you create immediate change; it's also to help you get to a clear, incredibly empowered place where you can continue learning, expanding upon, and practicing the skill of happiness for years to come.

Thanks so much for taking the time to step up and step out on this happiness adventure! We're in this together, and I'm so grateful to be making the journey with you. Stay open, be willing, stick with it relentlessly, and love yourself through it all. If you do, you'll create happiness, energy, positivity, and love that will stay with you through thick and thin for the rest of your life. Sounds pretty amazing, right? That's because it is.

PART I

THE BIGGER PICTURE: CHANGE YOUR VIEW OF HAPPINESS

CHAPTER 1

My Story . . . and Major Perception Changes

As I was sitting in my light-filled studio recently, working long hours on the proposal for this book, I received an urgent text from my brother Scott.

Scott: Are you sitting in front of your computer?

Me: Yes.

Scott: I'm sending you a link and then calling you.

Seconds later, the phone rang. Before I could say hello, he asked anxiously, "Did it come? Click on the link!"

"What is it?"

"Just open the link!"

I clicked, and a page with a photo of a joyful-looking couple appeared, along with a news article announcing that they had made a contribution to a local charity. I blinked twice, without the faintest idea why he was sending me this completely random, albeit positive piece of information.

"Are you looking at the link?" he asked.

I was shaking my head. I wanted to get off the phone and back to writing. "Yes, what is it?"

He launched into words that would permanently change the dynamic of my family.

"That's Mom's biological sister. Our aunt. And I just got off the phone with her."

My breath halted.

"At first, she didn't believe what I was telling her, that she had a sister and that I'm her nephew, but I sent her copies of records and some photos, and she definitely believes me now. And . . . Mom's mother is alive and well at eighty-eight years old."

Suddenly, I felt like I was in a lucid dream. My brain went into overdrive trying to sort out what this might mean for my family. It was a moment I thought would never happen. I'm talking *never.* I'd put the idea of ever being connected to that side of my family out of my mind and heart years ago. Sitting there in my old, worn office chair where I've spent countless hours writing, everything changed in an instant. My life, and the lives of my mother and brother, were forever shifted.

My mother was born in 1946, just after the war. Her mother was very young and couldn't keep her, so she gave my mother up for adoption. Although a wonderful, loving family raised my mother, she always had a deep desire to know where she came from. An embedded desire . . . on a cellular level.

Over the years, she had looked for her biological mother but, at some point, gave up on the idea and worked very hard to let it go, unwavering curiosity burning in a closed little box in her heart. Her mother went on with her life and kept the secret of my mother's birth for nearly sixty-seven years. Sixty. Seven. Years.

Growing up, I'd always wondered about it, too. It's strange to go through life knowing that you have another grandmother, a grandfather, and probably aunts, uncles, and cousins who have no idea you exist. But yet I, too, had tucked that wonder away in a box. I so strongly believed I would never know about that part of my family, I hadn't even thought about it for years.

My mother and her sister are beyond overjoyed to have found each other. It's been amazing to watch their meaningful, sisterly bond grow. Each had lost her other siblings and thought she was the last one surviving, until my brother connected them. Imagine . . . in midlife, after losing your siblings, discovering a wonderful sister you never knew existed! It's an amazing story. A miracle, really.

In the midst of these delicious events for my family, I found a powerful message. I believe I'm a wildly openhearted person and always do my best to carry a mind-set of *anything can happen. Anything.* I worked hard to adopt that mind-set, which has supported me greatly. Before I received that text from my brother, if you had asked me if there was anything—anything at all—I believed would *never* happen in my life, I probably would have answered absolutely not. *Never* is a word I don't particularly dig.

But with the unexpected discovery of my biological aunt and grandmother, I realized that this particular *never* was buried so deep, my belief about it so absolute, I didn't even realize it was there! If there was anything at all I truly believed would never happen, this was it. Never. Until it did.

I share this with you because it's a fantastic example of exactly what this first part of *Operation Happiness* is about: *changing your view.* Being willing to shift things you've firmly believed, or not believed, for your entire life.

You will begin to change your view by searching for and opening those boxes hidden within your heart that hold deeply embedded limiting beliefs about happiness and keep you from your most incredible life; you will have to be *willing* to replace those beliefs with new ideas and perspective. Give yourself the gift of a blank slate. It's the first step to creating a permanent, positive shift and opening yourself to an entirely new level of amazing.

Be open, be willing, clear your heart, and get ready to let a whole new light in.

"Give yourself the gift of a blank slate."

MY QUEST TO DECODE HAPPINESS

I truly love myself and my life. But believe me, it wasn't always that way. When I was growing up and all through my twenties, my life, for the most part, seemed like a consistent stream of struggle and mediocrity with a few highs here and there. But over the past twelve years, I've learned to embrace my truth as well as live by it. I've learned how to catch myself and make a shift when I'm stepping on my own toes and how to get out of my own way. I've stopped beating myself up and instead treat myself with understanding and compassion, knowing that I'm always doing the best I can. Most important, I've learned what happiness is and how to allow it to be the driving force of my life.

I wake up every morning filled with huge gratitude to finally be happy—and in complete control of my happiness. Along my path, I discovered a huge, life-altering truth about happiness, which I'm going to share with you in this chapter.

My own journey toward a permanent foundation for happiness that sustains and serves me daily was quite long. When I firmly decided at thirty-one years old that there had to be a better way to live, I dedicated myself passionately to studies of happiness, spirituality, and personal development, determined to change my life.

I made that decision in a definitive moment. It was early one cloudy, humid morning in the early summer of 2002, as I was once again lying in bed in a frustratingly dark place, absolutely dreading the day ahead. I'd been going through a ridiculously difficult time at work and within myself.

What I'd thought was my dream job had turned out to be a soul-crushing disappointment, and I felt like a cat stuck in a box, scratching and clawing with no way out. On top of it all, I was in the middle of planning my wedding and had all this crazy talk going on in my monkey mind: "Will he still want to marry me if I'm unemployed?" and "If I tell him I don't want this corporate job, fancy car, or fast-paced party life anymore, will he think I'm a fraud?" In many moments, it felt like every part of my world was literally imploding.

As I was lying there that morning, I received a loud message from within the center of my soul that, until hitting this wall of extreme darkness, I'd been unwilling to hear. The message was clear: In spite of everything that was causing my angst, frustration, and emotional pain at that time, the core foundation and creator of the problems was me.

Me? The problem? This was a new concept. How could I be the problem? I was a victim of circumstance!

But somehow, in that moment, I saw clearly for the first time that I was the major player, the MVP in fact, in every area my life, and if I chose to be, I could be in complete control. I had all the power in the world to create positive change, to escape the crazy, stressful situations I had chosen and continued to allow—and I hadn't been tapping into that power.

The only person who could change my world of gloom, mediocrity, and anxiety was me. I could choose to take leaps. I could choose to stop tolerating things that drained me or didn't bring me happiness. And I could choose to leave behind the sharks that had been circling me and swim with the angelfish instead.

It was a huge realization. I knew then that if I really wanted the best in life, it was time for me to look in the mirror, take responsibility for my own destiny, and *offer my very best back to life*. I had not been giving to the world what I wanted to receive.

I decided to find new strength, take charge, and do everything I could to make the shifts I needed to be happy and at peace, and to start living the life I knew I deserved. I had no idea where to begin, but I knew one thing for sure: There was a better way to live.

Until that morning that rocked my world, I'd been a young PR executive at a major entertainment studio. I had an office with a view of the Hollywood Sign, a gorgeous convertible, a huge wardrobe, a charismatic fiancé, and invitations to fantastic parties every week. On the outside, it seemed like I had an amazing life. I was convinced that I did have an amazing life, and that this must be how I was supposed to be living, because everyone told me how great it was. This is the life I'd been *conditioned* to strive for.

The truth was, even with all that great stuff going on, I was incredibly empty and unhappy inside, and I was very good at hiding it. I was so good, in fact, that the way I'd been surviving the tumultuous storm inside me was by working very hard to hide it from *myself*. I tried to remain in denial as much as I could. On some days, I couldn't deny it, and I would just wonder what on earth was wrong with me.

The corporate environment I was in at the time was highly toxic. I was working extremely long days and constantly dodging negative, venomous people. I was watching the few kind people around me either quit from the stress or get systematically pushed out for standing up for themselves. I spent most days lying low, wishing I were somewhere else.

Like many, I thought one of the answers to filling the emptiness was lots of stuff. I shopped like a crazy girl. I was making pretty good money for the first time in my life and was on a mission to find the next *thing* to make me happy.

I went to parties, polluted myself with too many cocktails, and burned the candle at both ends, thinking I was creating a great life for myself and, somehow, some way, it would lead to happiness. But it seemed that no matter what I did, I was unfulfilled. I was simply existing rather than living. The more I chased the wrong things, the emptier I felt. I wanted to be anyone but me.

One night, I was awakened by what felt like my heart exploding out of my chest. I was shaking and in a cold sweat. My pillow was soaked. I sprung up, took a few deep breaths, and realized I was reacting physically to the stress of my downward spiral. My body was finally telling me to wake the hell up or face major consequences.

The next morning, that wise inner voice spoke up (no, screamed) and finally opened my mind to see that I *had the power* to change my situation—and my perception—as long as I was willing to take responsibility for allowing it in the first place. I'm a creative person. Why wasn't I using that creativity to shape the life I truly wanted to live?

It was time to make some big changes, and that included going on an epic mission to discover exactly what it takes to be happy. I left the job. I had nothing else lined up; I just left and trusted that life would create a perfect opportunity. I only had enough money in savings for a few months' expenses, and I knew time would go quickly. It was the biggest leap of faith I'd ever dared to take. It was the first time I'd truly trusted the universe, and that changed everything.

I dropped all negative and draining obligations, stopped partying, gave away much of my stuff, and dove into every book and lecture I could find about transition, metaphysics, health, and happiness. I became fascinated with neuroscience and the power of the mind. I channeled all my newfound energy into learning, growing, making better choices, and creating a better life. I started my own boutique PR firm, empowered by the idea of working for myself on my own terms. Oh, and somewhere in the middle of all that, I got married. And no, he didn't think I was a fraud.

Over the next couple of years, I found so many conflicting views on what happiness is, how to achieve it, and how to sustain it, it made my head spin. With so much mixed information, some of it incredible and some of it complete crap, I felt called to set out on a quest to demystify happiness. To crack the code and simplify it in a way that I could fully understand and achieve happiness. It would be the journey of my life, and it would lead me to the work I do today.

So for a few years I kept at it. Making shifts, researching, growing. Many of the concepts and tools I learned did make a big difference. Through trial and error, weeding out the BS, and testing out some new theories of my own, I changed my life in powerful ways, reaching a higher level of peace and experiencing more frequent joy than I ever had before. It was a significant positive change. I couldn't believe how my world was turning around and how much I'd been missing. The more I changed my thoughts to be positive and loving, the more I cut myself a break and took the stance of self-compassion; the more I took action to create necessary lifestyle changes, the more I felt warmth and light fill my world.

But I knew in my gut there had to be more. I was still experiencing random, short bouts of depression and often felt apathetic about everyday events. I wanted to create a way of life that would bring a sustainable state of overall happiness and peace, a sense of daily enthusiasm, and give me more solid ground to stand on during the tough times.

I stayed on the course of my happiness mission over the next few years, continuing to filter things out, discovering what worked, and creating more positive changes. But I still didn't have a clear definition of happiness so it could be explained, understood, and realized. I was still looking for that "Hell yes! That's it!" moment. Then, in 2008, something sudden and unexpected happened that completely derailed my life, catapulted me into the most challenging battle I'd ever faced, and with it, brought a tremendous gift— the answers I'd been searching for.

The Fight That Brought the Light

I don't remember exactly how it happened that day when I was getting out of the bathtub. Maybe I was still loopy from the anesthesia or the painkillers and lost my balance. Maybe I slipped. Or maybe some part of me just felt the need to be on the floor for a while. The floor can sometimes feel like a comforting, safe place to cry.

I was cold and shaking, but my head felt hot. Instead of asking for help like a rational person who'd just had major surgery would, I decided, with one usable arm and legs I could barely stand on, to hoist myself out of the bathtub in the direction of the fluffy white towel on the counter. I wasn't thinking clearly, but I did know that after months of unrelenting, piercing pain, absent sleep, and inability to function physically the way I used to, my soul felt vacant—chewed up and scattered into nothingness. And it felt like my body was going with it.

Four months earlier, I'd woken up one morning feeling like someone had hit me in the shoulder with a large, heavy object. But I couldn't remember injuring that arm. Maybe I tweaked it in my sleep? I could barely move it, and when I tried to move even my fingertips, pain would shoot all the way up my arm and into my ear. I tried icing it, hoping it would improve, but by the next day, I couldn't move my shoulder, or my arm, at all. It felt like some humongous dude was literally holding my arm against my side and beating me with a heavy stick at the same time.

An orthopedic surgeon diagnosed me with a little-known condition called adhesive capsulitis. It's better known as frozen shoulder, which sounds much more docile than it actually is. It's a debilitating, mysterious disease that fuses the tissues and joint of the shoulder together, leaving a person in relentless, stabbing pain for months on end, unable to move the arm because everything has grown together. The medical community has no idea what causes it, and there is no cure. They speculate that it may be autoimmune. The only blessing is that for some unexplained reason, it resolves on its own somewhere between one and three years.

For many months, I couldn't do the most basic things I'd always taken for granted. The slightest movement was unbearably painful. I'd lost the use of my arm. Dressing myself, buttoning a shirt, driving, washing my hair, even just reading a book was physically impossible. Wow, do I appreciate these, and so many other things, every single second now!

Like many with this condition, I opted for surgery with the hope that it might speed up the healing process. No luck. Shortly after that, I found myself spread out on the frigid linoleum next to the tub.

I'm pretty sure the blaring, heaving sobs started on the way down. There must have been a thud, because my husband came running into the bathroom and was standing over me, a little stunned.

I glanced up at him, and even through my blurry tears I could tell by the look on his face that he really wasn't quite sure what to do with this sad, shattered creature. I watched him, in what seemed like slow motion, reach for the towel and begin to unfold it. Wet, shaking, and bruised, I somehow caught my breath enough to look up at him pleadingly and wail, "Why is this happening?" I'd hit bottom.

Later that night, lying in a blissfully cozy bed and still wrapped in the damp cotton towel, my thoughts finally were clear. A pack of frozen blueberries rested on my shoulder, creating a stark contrast against the warm sheets that felt strangely peaceful. I could hear "Satisfaction" by the Rolling Stones faintly playing from somewhere in the house and smiled at the irony. It occurred to me then that this was the first smile I had cracked in a long while, and it turned into a desperate-sounding giggle. I was so elated to feel this organic laugh pop out of me, more tears began to flow. I wiped them away with the towel, still smiling, and then a shift occurred that would finally get me headed in the right direction.

Nuzzling my head into the pillow and reflecting on the crazy drama from earlier that evening, I remembered the only sentence I'd been able to form in the middle of it: "Why is this happening?" That seemed like a legitimate question at the time. Who wouldn't ask it in that situation?

What happened next was a classic lightbulb moment. In searching for the answer, I realized that "Why is this happening?" was not the right question. The question I needed to be asking, which really in itself is the answer to the *why,* was "What can I learn from this?" I had learned through my metaphysical studies that this question is always effective in a crazy situation, because there is always something to learn. To be discovered. To be healed. It's a comforting question that can reveal a silver lining.

Lying in bed with the damp towel, a bag of ice-cold blueberries, and the Rolling Stones to console me, the question "What can I learn from this?" brought me to a major change in perception. I knew I had many months of physical therapy ahead and wouldn't be able to work much, if at all, during that time. I also knew being a caregiver was taking a toll on my husband, and the energy needed to shift. I decided to look at the time I had ahead of me as an amazing opportunity to focus all day, every single day, on finally decoding happiness. On becoming the super-healthy, peaceful, happy person I'd been working to be. I'd challenged myself to commit to it full-time, with absolute focus and intent. I was determined to heal my life and become a superstar version of me. Enter *Operation Happiness*!

Not long after I shifted to this new path, my body and spirit began to heal rapidly. I continued to study and practice everything I could when it came to happiness, healing, and whole living. I woke up every morning with the very deliberate intent to be happy that day. I indulged in my enthusiasm for connecting with nature by spending more time outside and gardening as part of my physical therapy. I switched to a mostly pescatarian diet (a diet that excludes meat, except for some seafood), started blending organic fruit and vegetable smoothies, and began checking out raw foods.

For quite some time, meditation, affirmations, and listening to lectures on healing and personal growth became the most important parts of my day. iTunes and my hot pink iPod were my new best friends.

After almost thirteen months, all the crazy hard work had paid off. I had most of the movement back in my arm, the pain had become bearable, and I could finally drive, work, and wash my own hair again. *Halle-freakin'-lujah!* Even better than all that, I felt like a completely new person. A happy person!

Soon I realized I absolutely *was* a new person. I was a person who'd created a successful foundation of habits, mind-sets, and daily activities that supported sustainable, authentic happiness even through the darkest days. And I was totally blown away by it.

After I'd recovered from all the health hurdles and settled back into my regular daily life, I began to notice that the happiness I was feeling wasn't wavering. Every day, I was living naturally in a state of positivity, joy, and ease. Without much thought, I was kind to myself, living an overall healthier existence, and pausing regularly and deliberately to take notice and find amazement in cool little stuff that had seemed so ordinary before. There were no more "space-between" gaps with crappy-for-no-reason days or weeks. It was just a peaceful, stable, seemingly permanent happiness that was naturally present within me every day. That's not to say there were no crappy-for-*good*-reason days, but I was handling even those days amazingly well with completely different thought patterns and actions. It was an entirely new energy and way of being. It all seemed to be coming so easily.

At that point, I knew I had something. I took a big step back and looked closely at my journey of the past year. What specific changes had I made that brought me to this new way of life? What had *finally* made the difference?

I wanted to figure this out precisely so I could stay in this great place. And it occurred to me that others might be interested in what changes I'd made as well. I'm a huge believer that when you find an awesome, effective solution to a common problem, you should grab a megaphone and shout it out! Right?

After digging in and checking out what seemed to finally support me in my newfound place of daily joy, I narrowed it down to three powerful shifts. Three. It all began to add up. Those three key shifts in perfect combination led to a permanent *foundation* to support my happiest, most incredible life. They led to a complete reprogramming of my mind-sets and habits. *This* is what had always been missing. Together those shifts permanently changed my life for the better. It's my heart's desire to walk you through the same three shifts in this book.

Operation Happiness is my megaphone.

This leads me back to what I mentioned at the beginning of this chapter, and the point of this chapter: *changing your view*. Changing the way I viewed happiness was the first of the three key shifts that created overwhelming change. After all, incredible transformation always begins with a change in perspective.

THE MISSING LINK TO HAPPINESS

So how exactly did I *change my view* of happiness? Well, during that year of recovery from the shoulder debacle, I was making a daily, conscious, and deliberate effort to live happiness once and for all. Basically, I just applied all the most valuable skills and happiness concepts I'd learned over the past few years on an enormous prevailing level. Happiness caffeinated.

It started a bit rough, almost like trying to squeeze on jeans that are too tight. Getting up in the morning and focusing so hard on happiness even felt uncomfortable at times because I wasn't used to making it my absolute number-one priority.

In the beginning, I was waking up with a sigh and strongly nudging myself to do things I hadn't done on a regular basis before. Short meditations; yoga poses; eating super-clean, nourishing foods; catching and correcting negative thought patterns; using positive affirmations. I immersed myself 24/7 in happiness habits and practices.

You know how they say the best way to learn a new language is to immerse yourself in it? Well, that's exactly what happened. After a few months of daily, conscious, forceful effort to create new habits, change my mind-sets, and make the things that brought me joy a top priority, a giant shift took place within my core, and it all started to come naturally. Every day, I was living on a foundation of consistent happiness habits, practices for inner peace, and supportive, positive mind-sets that came with ease and little effort. It no longer felt uncomfortable, and it no longer felt like work.

This led me to a *major* realization that was so incredible it literally changed me at the core: *Happiness is a skill.*

Yes, happiness is widely known as a choice, a feeling, a state of being . . . overlooked, it's actually a skill that can be learned, cultivated, and mastered—just like playing the violin or riding a bike.

The skill of happiness—just like playing an instrument—is made up of many facets and habits we can *learn*. Embracing and following this simple idea is profoundly life-changing. And once we learn the skill of happiness, just like any other skill that we learn, practice, and become good at . . . that's it! The hardest part of the journey is over.

Happiness is the required skill for living our very best life that they forgot to teach us in school. Think about it this way. If playing the violin were mandatory to thriving and living our best life, wouldn't you be kind of pissed if you'd graduated high school without learning how? And if you didn't discover this fact about the violin until you were, say, in your thirties or forties, would you beat yourself up for not knowing how to play? Of course not! Because nobody taught you while growing up or even told you this was a skill you needed! You'd pick up a violin and sign up for lessons ASAP, right? It's time we begin to look at the skill of happiness in this way and make it a higher priority, both in our lives and in society.

> "Happiness is the required skill for living our very best life that they forgot to teach us in school."

This is an extraordinary realization for all those who have struggled for years, frustrated and wondering why they haven't had sustainable, lasting happiness. Like me until my late thirties, they simply never learned *how to do it*. This one astonishing concept is the missing link that's been holding so many back from creating the happiness they desire.

Consciously cultivating and actively creating our own happiness is perhaps our most vital life skill. It's the foundation for all that is wonderful. What we're traditionally taught is most important—career, financial success, relationships—is nothing without it.

When I finally understood this, I felt a bit heavyhearted that I'd gone my entire life until that point lacking the most important skill. Growing up, we learned how to add and subtract, how to read, and the table of elements, but our well-meaning educators skipped the most important subject for thriving in this world: how to create a lasting, permanent foundation for happiness. They forgot to teach us! Perhaps because they never learned themselves.

In understanding this, I had a moment where I felt like Molly Ringwald in *Sixteen Candles* when she says, "I can't believe this. They fucking forgot my birthday!" Only to me it was, "I can't believe this. They fucking forgot to teach me how to be happy!"

I soon realized it wasn't that they actually forgot. It was that we've gone generation after generation neglecting to make this essential life skill part of what we teach our kids. Basically, the adults in our lives when we were growing up hadn't been taught either.

Imagine what the world would look like if children were never taught mathematics in school, and they were all sent out into the world to figure it out for themselves. Really . . . think about this. What would happen over a number of decades to advancement? Science? Business? I believe the absence of a curriculum on happiness and emotional health in schools has had a massive and unfortunate impact on our lives and on the world.

So there you have it. Begin now to think of happiness not just as a choice, a feeling, or a state of mind . . . but as a *skill*. A skill that can be learned, practiced, and even for the most part mastered. It's a required skill. It's also a *way of life*.

In my research, I came across a quote from the Greek philosopher Aristotle that perfectly illustrates happiness as a skill. In fact, it's part of what helped me focus on the incredible significance of this concept.

"*Happiness is a state of activity.*"

This is a tremendously powerful thought. Thinking of happiness as something we *do*, as something we actively participate in creating, rather than something we simply feel, can change the way we approach our happiness and our lives.

This is another big perception shift; happiness is absolutely a feeling and a state of well-being, but the key to happiness is understanding that it is created through action. And learning the *skill* of happiness helps us to consistently and naturally take the actions to shape and live our happiest, most dynamic life.

> " . . . *happiness is absolutely a feeling and a state of well-being, but the key to happiness is understanding that it is created through action.*"

Two kinds of action, or activity, are involved in the skill of happiness. The first is action we take within ourselves emotionally and spiritually. This includes consciously and deliberately choosing our thoughts (just like we would select an outfit for a night on the town); tuning in to connect with our inner voice and our bodies; meditating; and changing our default outlook so that we're always (or nearly always) consciously and unconsciously seeking joy, love, beauty, and light in everything around us. This is where it all begins.

The second involves physically doing things, even the smallest things, that consistently renew and refuel our happiness and well-being. The list of activities that can spark happiness is endless and different for everyone. The secret is for each individual to consciously recognize exactly which activities fuel their happiness flames and to add them to their toolbox.

As you move through the rest of this book, give yourself the gift of a beginner's mind. A clean slate. Perhaps take a day or two after reading this chapter, or at least sleep on it, to clear your mind and start fresh in approaching and thinking about happiness. Close your eyes, feel light fill your heart, and let feelings of openness and willingness to do things differently bubble to the surface.

Through the three powerful shifts I've made to build my own happiness foundation, we will get you started in forming your own: a solid, supportive ground to start from each day in creating your most incredible, joyful life. If you're willing to commit to doing the work (just as you would if you were passionately learning a new language or computer application), your life will forever change. I can't promise it will be easy, but I can tell you that if you stick with it for as long as it takes you to feel the shift in your core, you will reach a magical new level of consistent, sustainable happiness.

You can start to make changes and apply new tools and ideas in this book right away, but the true breakthrough will come when you continue to practice them for many, many months beyond, just like I did for more than a year during my recovery. That's the secret. Do it until it feels natural. Until your entire way of life— your way of being—changes without much thought. You'll feel the shift in every cell when it happens, just like you feel a shift when something becomes a habit or when you realize you've finally got something down you've been trying to learn.

Think of your new skill of happiness just like brushing your teeth: You need do it consistently and deliberately every day, more than once, or else funky, rotten stuff will begin to sneak in.

Now that I have you thinking of happiness as a skill, in the next two chapters we're going to work on some additional perspective shifts, supportive mind-sets, and essential tools, all part of changing your view on a number of levels. This will become the base for the other two of the three major happiness shifts, *changing your mornings* and *changing your habits*.

I'm so excited to share all this with you. With all my heart, thank you so much for being here. The rest of this book is filled with awesome, life-changing spirit candy, and I'm ecstatic you're here to share it with me.

Will you do me a favor right now? Take a little break. Put this book down and go do something that makes you feel happy. Something small, whatever it may be. A bath, a great glass of wine, a ridiculous guilty-pleasure TV show. Whatever—as long as it makes you feel good and gives you a bit of time to digest the initial stages of thinking about happiness in an entirely new way.

We're going to create some amazing changes together!

CHAPTER 2

The Five Key Happiness Mind-Sets

I'm one of those rare people who can remember back to the very early days of their lives. It sounds crazy, I know, but I can literally remember learning to walk. I have a clear memory of puttering around alone in my grandparents' trailer at one year old in my pale yellow walker with colored beads across the front, curious about the world. I remember pushing myself with my tiny hand off the wood paneling of the lower cabinets, attempting to make my way toward the door so I could scoot outside to where I heard the sounds of my parents and grandparents talking.

As I pushed back off the cabinet, I lost my footing, along with control of the walker, and awkwardly tumbled right out the door, down the step, and onto the ground. I let out a high-pitched wail, of which I can still hear the sound. I was a little banged up, but serious injury had been eluded, thankfully. My grandmother quickly ran over and picked me up, attempting to soothe me with her touch and voice. The last thing I remember from that scenario, funny enough, is the sound of them all arguing. Of course, I have no idea what they were saying; I just remember the tone and the chatter. Very likely a heated discussion about who was to blame for my calamity.

What's really nuts is that I can remember what I was thinking throughout this entire episode, kind of like the way you remember what you were thinking in one of those super-clear dreams. We honestly don't give babies enough credit. They're very aware of what's going on around them, they can employ logic, and they have a loud inner voice. I recall the actual thought—and feeling—I had the moment I lost my footing and realized I was going to roll out the door. It was something along the lines of . . . "Oh, shit!"—only it was more like "Wha-a-a-a-a!" since I didn't have complex language skills yet, but it meant the same thing.

What really blows me away about the walker debacle is not the memory of the scary moment when I fell out the door, but the minute or two before that, when I was just pushing myself around peacefully. Seriously, when I really think about this, it gives me chills! I can recall a few moments of my pure, clear, serene state of mind. A feeling of complete wonder and curiosity about the world. No stress. No past. No judgments. No pain. No fear. No limits. Just love.

When we're young children, this is our natural state of being. But as life unfolds and things happen, we largely lose touch with our true, pure nature of peace, wonder, joy, and love. Few people ever make it back anywhere close to that miraculous, unadulterated state. That's the path I'd like to illuminate in this chapter. Not just to discuss the ideas of love, forgiveness, compassion, kindness, and the fact that anything is possible—we're all aware that these are wonderful and powerful—but to have a meaningful conversation about how we can *become* them. This is where the real magic happens.

YOUR BRAIN IS YOUR BFF

Let's get scientific for a minute and chat about a wildly amazing miracle called *neuroplasticity*. In a way, it's your key to everything this book is about. Learning how this works was one of my biggest breakthroughs in fully understanding exactly how one can go about creating lasting, sustainable happiness, love, and inner peace. It has everything to do with the way our brains work.

The simple way to explain neuroplasticity is that it's your brain's ability to change its programming in your synapses (signal transmitters) and neural pathways (information vehicles). This occurs through deliberate and consistent changes in your thoughts, behaviors, emotions, physical habits, and even your environment. In other words, you are in control. You can literally *undo* years of negative limiting programming and rewire your brain's default, automatic settings to happiness and positivity! Yes, you can! Isn't that incredible?

Much of what they taught us about our brains in science class has been overturned in the past couple of decades, and researchers have discovered astonishing scientific evidence that the old saying "You can do anything you set your mind to" is actually true!

Scientists once believed that after our first few years, our brains were basically set and would function and remain largely the same for the rest of our lives. But that old-school way of thinking has been changed by extensive research that shows our brains are constantly changing and by the amazing realization that we can control and take charge of many of those changes on multiple levels, even down to our cells.

When I learned about neuroplasticity and then linked it with the profound transformation I experienced through dedicating myself completely to happiness and positive change while recovering from my illness back in 2008, it all fell into place. Through resolute dedication and a series of deliberate, positive, consistent changes in a number of areas, you can transform your life into a happy, supportive, joy-filled place. It's a scientific fact. How extraordinary!

> *"Through resolute dedication and a series of deliberate, positive, consistent changes in a number of areas, you can transform your life into a happy, supportive, joy-filled place."*

This is amazing, life-changing news for anyone who has ever felt like they just weren't "wired" for consistent, lasting happiness. You can completely rewire your natural state and default mind-sets to automatically operate from a foundation of happiness, peace, love, and positivity. We all have the power to create our own beautiful brain makeover!

In one study conducted by researchers from Massachusetts General Hospital, sixteen participants spent eight weeks in a mindfulness-based stress-reduction program at the University of Massachusetts Medical School Center for Mindfulness. They went to weekly meetings, which included a practice of mindfulness meditation (focusing on nonjudgmental awareness of feelings, sensations, and state of mind). They also practiced mindfulness exercises daily on their own using guided meditation recordings for an average of twenty-seven minutes for the eight-week period. At the end of the study, the participants reported significant improvements.

When the researchers reviewed the MR (magnetic resonance) images taken of the brain structure of the sixteen participants two weeks before the study began and then again two weeks afterward, they found notable changes in the regions of the brain known to be important for learning, memory, self-awareness, compassion, empathy, and introspection. Participants also reported significant decreases in stress, which correlated with readings on the brain images that showed reduced gray-matter density in the amygdala, the part of the brain that plays a large role in anxiety, stress, and emotional reactions.

The people who took part in this study weren't just feeling significantly better because they'd been chilling out a lot (although as we know there's much to be said about ample time for relaxation and positive thinking); they actually changed their brains! Think about the power in that! No chemicals, no unrealistic lifestyle changes, no massive time commitment . . . and they literally created scientific transformation in the quality of their lives. The researchers also suggested that longer-term effort with the mindfulness practices could result in even more positive changes.

You don't need to take part in a study to start working on this for yourself; just your own Operation Happiness. By absolutely knowing that through consistent practice and unwavering dedication to the ideas, tools, and concepts in this book that resonate with your heart, and through others you'll discover on your journey, you'll create incredible changes in the way your brain works that will support you in extraordinary ways for the rest of your life. Any limiting beliefs about the way you're wired, your ability to change, and the power your brain has to shape your world are just that—limiting beliefs. The truth is that your brain is a beautiful, remarkable, malleable miracle—and with few exceptions, you're in charge.

With conscious effort, practice, and consistent, deliberate intention, it's possible to bring ourselves to an empowered place where we largely embody and *naturally operate from* the key happiness mind-sets we'll chat about in this chapter: *love, forgiveness, compassion, kindness,* and *anything is possible.* A truly light-filled way of being. Ready to get going? Let's do this!

THE IMPORTANCE OF GRATITUDE

Before we get into the five key happiness mind-sets, I want to share with you a bit on gratitude. Gratitude is a magical, tangible daily practice that can transform your life, elevate your positive energy, and support your happiness like nothing else can. It's not just about being thankful; living in a perpetual state of gratitude is an actual state of being. It's a way of life so powerful it amplifies all joy, love, forgiveness, compassion, and a panoply of other brilliant treasures.

Gratitude multiplies gratitude, so the more you allow yourself to feel grateful for things in your life—good and bad, large and tiny—the more gratitude you will feel running through your veins. You can actually feel a physical shift inside when you enter a state of deep gratitude. Once you become accustomed to that shift, you'll want to be in that space as often as possible. It truly is one of the best experiences on earth, and we can create it anytime we choose.

Gratitude is a powerful thread connecting all the key happiness mind-sets. It can support and magnify each one to bring them to their highest levels. As you dive into the rest of this chapter, I encourage you to begin cultivating deep gratitude—really feeling it—and allowing it to unfold within you like a grand flower blooming.

A great way to do this is to keep a gratitude journal. In it, write down a few things each day you're grateful for. It could be several things, or just one or two you want to focus on that day. This is a luminous, transformative practice. In fact, I would even suggest putting this book down for a few minutes and starting one right now. It will help open you more fully to creating the shifts we'll talk about in this chapter, and it will serve as an opportunity to pause and recognize how truly amazing this life is. Joy rises from gratitude.

Now we'll dig in! I encourage you to view the vital mind-sets outlined here as your *elements in a new way of being*—a new lifestyle of default settings that your heart and mind will automatically turn to for insight and guidance in all scenarios. The objective is to practice shifting to them at every opportunity, even when it feels uncomfortable, until they become a dominant part of the natural way your mind works. This will not just expand the presence of these mind-sets within your brain and your heart, but it will also help to edge out some of the old mind-sets and limiting beliefs that have been hindering your happiness up until now. It will essentially change the lens through which you see the world.

We'll start with love. Like gratitude, love is a through line that can support the other mind-sets, which is why it's first and also why I write the most about it. *Love is the single most powerful force in the universe.*

HAPPINESS MIND-SET #1: LOVE

Love is the most remarkable, pure, empowering place to live from. Do all things from a place of pure love, and your world will change profoundly.

Acting and Reacting from a Place of Love

It's so easy to act and react from places other than love, when the truth is that love is the most important part of the foundation of every single thing we do. Actions without a foundation of love lack positive momentum and energy and are almost always clearly noticeable, yet they are common. Some examples include snapping at a loved one for leaving socks on the floor, verbally or mentally beating ourselves up for any reason, or criticizing someone starting with words like "You always . . ." and "Can't you just . . . . " Creating a shift to consistently act from love—most if not all of the time—is where to begin rewiring your energy and anchoring your foundation for happiness.

This may be a bit of a challenge at first. I remember a time when, although love was present in my life, my default places to start most anything were fear, anxiety, fatigue, or apathy—not the greatest places to live or act from. The good news is that I discovered through my journey that the more we teach ourselves to practice living and acting from love, as well as from the other mind-sets outlined in this chapter, the less room there will be for unwanted negative states to creep in, and the more we'll notice them and give them the boot when they do.

Think of your mind (and even your whole life!) as a closet. In this book, we're basically looking to clean out all the stuff that no longer fits or serves you and fill those spaces with fabulous things that suit you perfectly and make you feel amazing. We're going to shift the vibes from which you operate.

Begin each morning by consciously shifting into and very deliberately remaining in a loving mind-set toward every action and interaction, and especially toward yourself. Gently correct your course when you feel yourself shifting away from it. This will profoundly change the way you experience your life and the way others experience you.

Dedicate yourself long enough to doing this with great awareness on a daily basis, and you will build the default mind-set of love naturally and with ease. You'll likely even feel a physical shift in your being. You'll begin to notice shifts in the way you think about and view different things, including other people. Believe it or not, some people who used to really annoy you may not be so annoying anymore, because you're looking at them from a place of love and acceptance rather than *expecting* that they're going to be annoying or that they should in some way be different. Some of your longtime core beliefs may even shift, and some of your priorities likely will, too.

Here's an example. My good friend Lisa called me to share that a woman in her office was driving her absolutely bananas. "I can't stand her! She's so mean to everyone!" Lisa was totally stressed out because this woman's attitude was making it hard for her to get up and go to work in the morning. She asked me for advice.

"Does she seem like a happy person?" I asked, already knowing the answer.

"Hell no! She's grouchy and negative. I don't even know why they keep her working there. She makes negative comments and nitpicks at everyone's faults."

"It sounds to me like this woman is very unhappy and may be really hurting inside," I said. "What if she's desperate for love and acceptance, and she's stuck in a cycle of negativity and anger because she's full of sadness, resentment, and lack of self-love?" I gave Lisa a few seconds to ponder this.

"Wow. I never thought of it that way. That's kind of sad. She always looks tired and, yeah, under all that crap, she does seem more sad than angry, I think."

I gave her a little challenge. "Okay, this might be hard at first, but just go with it. Tap into feeling love and compassion in your heart for this woman, who is clearly in pain. Sometimes, the people who are hardest to love are the ones who need it most. Try smiling brightly at her first thing tomorrow morning and pay her a compliment. If her response is bitchy, let it go like water off a duck's back. Bring her a tea or coffee and tell her about something she did recently that you really appreciated. When she's negative, respond with more loving-kindness. Don't do it in a kiss-ass way, but from a place of true compassion and sincerity. Try this for a few days and see if anything changes."

Lisa agreed but sounded doubtful. A few days later, she sent me a text: "OMG, it totally worked! She asked me if I wanted to go to lunch! She even cracked a joke and has been so much nicer. Better!"

> Text
> "*Sometimes, the people who are hardest to love are the ones who need it most.*"

Lisa's shift shows that approaching every situation and every action from a place of love and nonjudgment not only creates positive change in our own lives, but in the lives of those around us. It's an awesome ripple effect.

When you begin to shift to the default mind-set of love, the key is to literally embody love in every action and thought pattern. It may seem weird at first to see brushing your teeth or making yourself a sandwich as acts of love, but if you really think about them as things you're doing to care for yourself, they absolutely are.

So when you're doing simple, everyday things or having simple, everyday conversations, focus mindfully on the love and magic behind them. Invite love into each and every space and intent. Notice the way you feel at your core after you've done this for even a short time; the change will amaze you.

Giving and Receiving Love

For my entire life, until my own transformation and awakening, I'd focused on just a few kinds of love. Family love, romantic love, love between friends, love for the animals in my life, and maybe a bit of self-love mixed in now and then, although not nearly enough. What I didn't know about at the time, and what I was totally missing out on, was the massive well of love that is available to all of us outside those parameters if we open ourselves to it and train our minds and hearts to remain open. The light, joy, and support available from that well of love truly never ends.

So how do we tap into the love outside the lines we're conditioned to think within? *We expand our view of what defines love.*

We look for and feel the love in everyday occurrences and actions and allow ourselves to fully experience it. We begin to see and fully embrace infinite love all around us, even in the smallest things.

For example, letting someone who's clearly in a hurry go in front of you in line in the grocery store can be seen as not just an act of courtesy, but of love. It really is. People feel loved most when they feel seen, heard, and accepted.

You can feel loved when a stranger smiles at you or says hello and share love by doing this for others throughout your day. It's not just for them; it's for you. Small acts of love and vibrations of love surround us. If we let ourselves fully open to it and consciously experience it, we can actually bathe in it. How awesome is it to live from *that* place?

Recently, on a cool fall morning, I walked out into my garden for some fresh air and spotted a bright pink cosmos flower blooming. It was the middle of October, yet here was this beautiful bloom reminiscent of summer to greet me! How very cool! I walked over to admire it and, of course, posted a picture to share with friends. Then I stood there and really took the time to marvel. Nature is truly filled with love, and there are signs of it everywhere. *Cosmos* is a Greek word meaning "balanced universe." I chose to see this little cosmos bloom as a sign of love from the universe. A gift of love from the garden to which I give so much love and care. A reminder of that infinite well. My choice to see it that way made it so.

All things can be seen with love. Gratitude is a tremendous expression of love. Kindness is love. Nature is love. Small, everyday actions are love. Even rejection is love. (Think of it as the universe's way of filtering out what's not right for you.) And at our center, we are love.

Here's a little exercise to help you start receiving, expanding, and giving *all* the love that is possible in your life. Try spending an entire day loving everything and everyone, without exception. Begin with loving your bed. Seriously! (That's an easy one.) Love yourself. Love your family. Love the postal delivery person. *Love that person who is hard to love.* Love your body. Love the checkout guy at the grocery store. Love the bags he puts your groceries in. Love the barking dog that lives next door. This is not as easy as it sounds, but with practice, it will begin to flow naturally. Radiate love. . . be open to receiving love . . . consciously choose love in every moment. See how this profoundly shifts your energy. Then repeat this daily, over and over again, until it doesn't seem like effort anymore. Until you feel an intense shift within—a love reprogramming!

Seeing the Love in Difficult Situations

Some anger, resentment, and frustration can even be seen as love. This is huge, because when we're able to do this, it changes everything. This was the hardest thing for me to wrap my head around, but when I began seeing the love beneath everything, including the seemingly negative, my heart ached with joy. As with Lisa's story about the woman in her office, looking for a love-based explanation in every situation is incredibly powerful and can shift outcomes in amazing ways.

This perspective changed so many of the stories I'd been repeatedly telling myself about past events in my life. People act out of their need for love, out of the love they feel, or out of fear, which ultimately is fear of not being loved. Once I fully understood this, I saw so many things from a totally new standpoint. I could see that many of the people I thought had hurt or abandoned me were actually acting in some way from a place of love.

I'll share a personal story that's a great example. During my senior year of high school, I fell wildly in love with a guy I'd worked with as a camp counselor over the previous summer at the local YMCA. To me he was everything. Our friendship, our connection, and the way my heart swelled with love when I looked at him or heard his voice—it was off the charts. It was my first great romantic love and, to this day, is one of the most significant loves of my life. We spent our senior year essentially growing up together, laughing with friends, spending late nights under the stars, and engaging in deep conversations about life and what we thought we wanted.

Then, just before graduation, he broke it off. I can still remember clearly the way my heart exploded in agony when he kissed me on the arm, a piece of his wavy hair falling into his eye and pain in his voice as he said goodbye and stepped out of my car. I was absolutely shattered. And at that young age, I had no idea what to do with that.

Every breath felt like needles in my chest when the graduation ceremony came and I walked down the stage in my cap and gown, feeling like my world was ending instead of just beginning. Yeah, I had a pretty lame graduation, to say the least.

It took several years before I no longer writhed over the loss. I didn't understand how he could walk away when it seemed he loved me the same way I loved him. I was confused, my trust in life shaken, and everything I thought was real about love had been broken.

Although we'd stayed in touch as friends on and off over the years, I went for more than twenty-three years without answers, always a little sting nagging at me whenever I'd remember those times. In the summer of 2012, a conversation with him over a friendly drink one night revealed a powerful, story-altering truth that I'd never considered before.

He didn't leave me all those years ago because he didn't love me. *He left because he did.*

That night, we'd ended up out at a local pub after many years of not hanging out, mostly to catch up and talk about how life was going. It was special to both of us that we'd kept in touch for so long. After a couple of hours of laugher and cathartic conversation, I felt that the door had finally opened for me to ask the question that had lived in my heart for so long.

"So, can I ask you something?" I asked, allowing a wave of courage to swell inside me. "Were you ever in love with me?"

I knew he'd be honest. Why not at this point? It wouldn't affect our friendship either way. I braced myself for "I thought I was, but . . . . " Instead it was an entirely different conversation.

"Of course I was!" he replied.

Surprised, a notable lump forming in my throat, I asked, "Then why did you leave?"

He tilted his head and looked at me, curiously, revealing a tiny ember of the light in his eyes that I'd fallen for all those years ago. "Don't you know?" he asked.

"What?! No, I have no idea!"

"We were way too young for what we had. There was nowhere to go from there! What were we going to do, get married at seventeen? Hell no. We were stuck. There really wasn't any other choice, as much as that sucked."

Whoa! Stop the presses! I'd never thought of it that way. He was absolutely right. How wise he was, even at seventeen. I was floored. The pain I'd carried for all those years immediately dissolved. I felt a positive, physical shift within myself. If I'd just been willing to look at things differently, *to see the possibility of love as the foundation of his actions in the first place*, it would have changed everything. This answer was so clear all along; I'd just never been willing to look closely enough. He wasn't tossing me aside all those years ago . . . he was setting us both free.

Holy moly! Talk about a big shift and a brand-new version of the story! We're still dear friends to this day.

Are there painful stories in your life where you might shift your view to see the love that was there all along? The true foundation of someone's actions, even if you didn't agree with them? A falling out with a friend or family member? A past heartbreak? Something you haven't yet forgiven yourself for when you were really only acting in some way out of love? When you do this, you may surprise yourself with some of the realizations you'll have.

Through this process, you will feel pain lift away, and that space in your heart where the pain used to live will be filled with peace and understanding. I don't usually encourage digging up the past, but when it has something new to say (which isn't often), it's worth it! When you're armed with a new perspective, sometimes launching an excavation to mine past experiences for new versions of the stories or alternative explanations can be life-changing. Once true clarity is reached, you can finally let go once and for all.

Permanently shifting your view to see the love beneath nearly all situations will also change the way you see and experience difficult situations that may arise in your future. It takes practice to regularly pause and deliberately look for the love, especially in very emotional scenarios. Sometimes, it takes willingness to look in the mirror to see your part. It can be like playing hide-and-seek. But with continued effort, you'll begin to see through the lens of love, which will open incredible new doors, flood your world with light, and offer a magical new vista.

Love and Our Passions

The summer I turned three, I planted a handful of watermelon seeds in my backyard sandbox to see if they would grow. Each morning for several days, I ran out to water them with water I'd scoop out of the pool and to check for sprouts. I vividly recall the magical morning when the first sprout was waiting to greet me. The instant I spotted it, I was bubbling with excitement and wonder in complete and total awe of nature and life. To me, that little sprout literally sparkled.

That experience with the watermelon seeds was filed away with thousands of other life experiences, and although I didn't know it at the time, it became part of who I am. In a way, the single moment when the seed sprouted in my sandbox became a seed itself. Thirty years later, I discovered I had a soulful passion for gardening. When I discovered this passion, the memory of how I felt as a child when that seed sprouted in my sandbox came flooding back, and it all made complete sense. It's now become a beloved hobby that brings me tons of joy and childlike giddiness, and ties into my passions for organic living and growing my own food.

The things we're passionate about are an extension of love in our lives. Seeing our passions as another form of giving and receiving love can magnify the purpose and joy they give us. This is also part of the reason why it's so uplifting to listen to people talk enthusiastically about something they're passionate about—it's completely contagious. Pure love. I could listen all day to someone talking about watching paint dry if it was infused with infectious, ridiculously zealous passion and joy.

One of the things I hear most when coaching clients or speaking to groups is that they feel like they lack passion in their lives. At times I've felt that way, too, so I completely relate. It's heartbreaking to think that some people live that way for very long periods, even years. But it's never too late to bring back the zing.

One of my first suggestions for cultivating more passion is to create a list of early childhood memories that filled you with joy and wonder, like my memories of the watermelon seeds. See if you can link those experiences to anything present in your life now or anything you've been desiring to invite into your life. You might find a few surprises. The links don't have to be too literal. Maybe you loved playing house when you were young and now you long to work in interior design.

We discover many of our true passions and innate gifts when we're kids but lose our connection to so many of them as we get older. Sometimes, the things you're really passionate about are already a part of your life; they just need to be recognized and nurtured to start really burning. They're present as sparks that will allow you to build intense fires when you're ready.

Passion doesn't have to link to just one or two big pursuits in your life. It can be infused into nearly everything if you consciously allow it to be, just like love. They go hand in hand. You can find passion in the artistic way you make your coffee in the morning, if you look.

A simple way to start enjoying more passionate energy is to slow down just a bit to mindfully focus much more on the pleasures of everyday sensory experiences. When sipping a glass of wine or a great tea, or taking a bite of food, allow yourself to be fully present to the taste, feel, and sensation. Feel the gratitude in your heart for that single taste or bite. This practice can turn even tea and a scone into a five-star dining experience.

If you're viewing a beautiful work of art or just putting on a favorite coat, really marvel at the details of these small miracles. Notice the brushstrokes or the stitching. Vocalize your feelings more often to create full presence and to share that energy with those around you. Isn't it delicious when you hear someone say something passionately, like "Oh, wow! This is *the* most incredible cheese I've tasted in forever! Have you tried it?" Makes you want to race to take a bite, doesn't it?

Try this sensory adventure for thirty days and see how it elevates the passion, pleasure, and love energy in your life. Not to mention this kind of energy is super-sexy on every level! Other people will find it contagious. It may seem over the top at first, but you'll find a balance that's comfortable for you, and it will make a tremendous difference in the way you experience and enjoy everyday things. Keep it going deliberately for at least the thirty days I suggest here, and it will become an effortless part of how you go about things. It will also help you discover some of the larger passions that could lead you down amazing new roads.

Romantic Love

I wish I'd learned much earlier that authentic, delectable romance can be found in many, many places. Not just with a significant other. Merriam-Webster currently defines romance as "an emotional attraction or aura belonging to an especially heroic era, adventure, or activity." Oxford says romance is "a quality or feeling of mystery, excitement, and remoteness from everyday life." (No wonder I have an immediate mad crush on every boat I lay eyes on!) How cool is that? We can tap into an endless number of things to evoke those feelings and experiences.

The previous section on passion is a great example: Romance can be nearly everywhere you look, if you choose to see it. Our natural longing for romance can be satisfied regularly if we seek the romance in everyday pleasures and in *all* our relationships.

Romance can be found and enjoyed in relationships with friends and family members. It can be shared with people with whom we have a common passion—even with coworkers. It can be experienced sitting under a tree alone enjoying an afternoon breeze, or on a solo date night with candles, a great meal, and the TV remote. It's present in everything we love to do.

Shifting our view to see the romance available from so many sources (just like the love that's available from so many sources) will help fill that part of our spirits that longs for those feelings. And in a relationship with a significant other, tapping into romance, love, and passion from other sources can help keep sparks present as well. That energy, when truly embraced, can't help but spill into and elevate all areas of life.

Now, in the area of relationships with romantic partners, I can honestly tell you that, like many, I've had to learn huge lessons by screwing up, falling on my face a few times, experiencing enormous heartbreak, and, in spite of it all, working to keep the faith.

A loving, soulful relationship with a significant other can be an amazing gift and can certainly add to our happiness—"add to" being the key idea to consider. One of the biggest mistakes I've made in past relationships, and I know many can relate to this, is allowing my own happiness to depend on the actions and approval of the other person. This is backward and ultimately unfair to the person on whom we're placing that responsibility—that's a lot of pressure!

The truth is, the way we can show up as our very best and offer the greatest amount of love and support to our partner is to take complete responsibility for our own happiness, from A to Z. The purpose of a love relationship is not to fill a void, to complete us, or even to be part of the foundation for our happiness. Its purpose is to help us grow emotionally and spiritually and to enhance an already full, happy life. This is a key standpoint from which joyful, lasting relationships survive, thrive, and grow.

Growing your happiness is virtually guaranteed to significantly improve your love life as well. So I'm going to share with you a few of the profound lessons I've learned that may greatly support you in cultivating a loving, soulful partnership. They apply not only to relationships with significant others but also to our passions, careers, and relationships with ourselves and those we love. These are things I now know for sure and would have loved to know when I was much younger. (It would have saved me a whole lot of grief!) They're ideas I consider exceptionally important in any happiness toolbox, as well as excellent bricks in a happiness foundation.

Staying in love is a choice. Falling in love is magical, amazingly significant, and a bit of a mystery, all in one beautiful package. We all know those couples who have been together for many years and still seem to be in love. You'll often hear people commenting on how wonderful it is or asking how they do it. The answer is *they choose it and then act on it*. Over and over again. Waking up each morning and choosing great love is part of what makes it so.

> *"Waking up each morning and choosing great love is part of what makes it so."*

Choosing to be in love involves consciously remembering why you first fell in love with your partner, purposefully focusing on the things you love about them (instead of little, insignificant faults), and deliberately tapping into the immense gratitude and happiness you feel because your partner is part of your world. This person is choosing to love you and walk the path with you, so allow yourself to be amazed and honored by this . . . every single day. Doing this empowers light, love, affection, and chemistry. Falling in love is beautiful magic; staying in love is a choice. And like so many incredible things in life, it requires action. Choose love every day.

• **Loving someone means supporting that person's freedom.** When we love someone, we like to think we know what's best for him or her. Sometimes we do. We also like to think they should make important choices while considering how it will affect our relationship. True, to a point. While it's great to share our insights, advice, and guidance with our partner out of love, we also have to allow the space for the one we love to make decisions based on what's calling their soul, and we have to support their choices— even when they're not our choices. Love does not try to control. Zen Buddhist monk, spiritual teacher, and author Thich Nhat Hanh says this beautifully: "You must love in such a way that the person you love feels free." Yes. And we must also be loved in such a way that we feel free.

The key to longevity in relationships is *acceptance.* When I was twenty-five, I was working as an assistant on a cable TV show about healthy lifestyles. I was in the green room one morning stuffing my face with a spring roll meant for the day's expert guest, sure he wouldn't miss one. As I finished chewing, a man walked in who had a beautiful, magnetic energy. I quickly swallowed and smiled at him.

I had no clue at the time who this man was or what he was all about, but I knew immediately that I wanted to listen to everything he had to say. His name was Deepak Chopra. He said good morning and I welcomed him, explaining a few logistics about what to expect on the set. He was warm and kind and seemed completely at ease. I had no idea at the time the huge impact his teachings would have on my life. You know those times when you look back and think, *"Damn! Wish I'd known!"*? That was one of those times for sure. He put his things down and began to settle in. "Do you need anything else?" I asked.

"No, I'm fine, thank you," he answered. Then he offered me a spring roll.

Fifteen years later, I was at a talk in downtown Los Angeles that Dr. Chopra gave to a group of women entrepreneurs about prosperity and success. Many great questions were asked that day about business and abundance. But one question asked of him was completely off topic, and I think the answer changed everyone in the room. A woman stood up and asked, "You have a long and loving relationship with your wife. What would you say is the secret to a lasting, happy relationship?" You could feel the energy shift as everyone leaned forward to hear his response.

There was a short pause as he thoughtfully decided on his answer. We expected to hear that the secret was love, communication, or patience. All very important, of course. But his profound and unexpected answer was a major *of course!* moment.

"Acceptance. Total acceptance."

The room was silent for a few moments, except for a few soft gasps and a couple of audible wows. Before I even knew what I made of it, I felt tears welling up in my eyes. In that moment, I realized that this vital ingredient had been missing from just about every relationship I'd ever been in, including my marriage. Holy crap.

This lesson permanently shifted the way I show up in every relationship in my life, including those with family and friends—even in my relationship with myself.

Acceptance

Complete and total acceptance! Absolutely! The most under-rated element in any loving, lasting relationship. We all grow and change over the years. Our dreams change, our bodies change, our opinions change. When we love someone and choose to make a life with that person, we must be willing to accept him or her just as they are. Without judgment. We must continue choosing to fully accept them every single day, just as we choose to be in love with them every day, and *just as we deeply desire to be fully accepted ourselves.* We must be open to growing together, or risk growing apart.

We have to be willing to love someone, flaws and all; love them through their mistakes, in spite of their habits that don't match ours; and learn to embrace imperfections as part of the total package of the person we love.

This doesn't mean it's not okay to give your partner loving encouragement and support to grow and make improvements. It means doing this while at the same time fully loving, supporting, and *accepting* that person exactly as they choose to be, and just where they are. Offering each other the gift of complete acceptance is a beautiful foundation for a loving relationship. It's never too late to begin fully and unconditionally accepting your partner, your-self, and all those who matter in your life. This is a tremendous and incredibly freeing act of love.

What's missing is what you're not giving. Oh, yeah! Personal responsibility! Ugh, it can be so uncomfortable. It's a tough one, but owning our own junk can bring astonishing awareness to our relationships and our lives, as well as positive change and clear answers. It's hugely empowering if you're willing to go there.

I learned this a while back in my studies of the metaphysical text *A Course in Miracles*. The course teaches that *only what you have not given can be lacking in any situation.* This is a monumen-tally powerful truth.

When I first heard this idea, I was like, "Whoa! What *I'm* not giving? I'm not sure about that one!" But the more I dove in and reflected on the deep meaning of this idea, and the more I opened myself to looking at what more I might be able to offer in different situations, the more I realized that what's missing in any situation is *always,* in some way, what I'm not giving.

Here's a tough but super-empowering statement if you're willing to embrace it: *Ongoing emotional suffering is our own doing.* It's never the responsibility of anyone else. The actions of others may contribute to our initial hurt, but choosing to continue to suffer and then blaming others for that ongoing suffering is just a way of evading responsibility for what we've created and allowed.

Now, sometimes, there's a very valid reason for ongoing emotional suffering, such as the loss of a loved one or another traumatic life event. In these cases, it's important to give yourself a loving amount of space and a reasonable amount of time to grieve. But I can honestly say that this, too, is an area where we must take responsibility at some point and be willing to move forward, heal, and rebuild. You may feel like life will never be the same after a great loss, and you're right. It will be different. But know that this doesn't mean it can't be full of happiness, love, and light again. You are deserving of this.

What's wonderful and so powerful about this is that when we fully understand its absolute truth, we know we always have the power to take action to move toward dissolving and releasing our suffering anytime we choose. We are in complete control. And the way to begin doing this is by giving more, loving more, and forgiving all. Taking personal responsibility is a tremendous act of courage.

If you've ever felt that "I've lost myself" or "I can't be myself anymore" in a love relationship, believe me, you're not alone. So many of us have been there—I know I have—and it can be a painful, damaging place, especially when we blame the other person (which happens all too often). You wouldn't blame your partner if you lost your keys, right? So why do we tend to blame others when we lose ourselves?

The truth is, only we are responsible for our own happiness, well-being, and emotional fitness. It's a huge mistake to put the key to your own happiness on someone else's keychain, not to mention totally unfair to that person. If you ever feel like you've lost touch with yourself, like you can't be yourself, or like "something's missing" in a relationship, begin working through it by asking what more you can give. Own your part. Take your power back. Dig deep. Really examine this, and the answers will surprise you.

This is not to say that every relationship has the potential to be healthy or right. What every relationship *is,* however, is an opportunity to learn and grow. In toxic or abusive situations, or when your inner voice is telling you this is not the partner for you, the part that is lacking may be acknowledgment of the fact that the relationship needs to come to an end. Therefore, the "*What more can I give?*" becomes the act of letting go. Walking away becomes an act of love, as does forgiving and viewing the other person with compassion.

Whatever you're looking for, begin by giving more. If you want more love, be more loving. If you want more understanding, be more understanding. If you want more affection, be more affectionate. Gush! And when it comes to intimacy, take action to get your sexy on! Act *as if* the fire is there, and the desire will appear. Give, give, give, and watch the sparks fly!

Self-Love

"energy is everything"
Sept. 18 19

Last spring, I visited Paris for the first time. Oh, I could write another whole book on my passionate love affair with that delicious city! I felt drenched in beauty and love every moment I was there.

One delightfully rainy afternoon, I was sitting in a café sipping white wine and watching incredibly interesting people walk by. A ruggedly sexy French guy who was sitting behind me struck up a conversation.

"How long are you here for?" he asked in a scrumptious, raspy voice with an accent that could melt steel.

"Only a couple more days, but I'm really wishing it was longer!" I answered smiling, momentarily euphoric that he spoke to me.

"You have a very special vibration about you," he said. "What do you do?"

Wow. A small reminder once again that energy is everything.

Something about his authentic, inquisitive tone told me he wasn't really flirting; he was looking for some company and interesting conversation. Truly. When I looked at his face again, I detected an underlying layer of genuine curiosity and sensed he'd been through many struggles in his days.

"I'm a life coach, writer, and speaker. I study and write about happiness."

Three Steps to Self-love

Consider these three steps to begin expanding your love for your incredible self.

1. **Treat your body, mind, and spirit like they belong to someone you love deeply.** Have you ever heard the saying that if we treated our friends the way we treat ourselves, we wouldn't have any friends? Kind of funny, I know—but also eye-opening. Treat yourself with love, kindness, and compassion like you are your very best friend in the world—like you are the *hero* of your life. *Because you are.*

2. **Start consciously seeing even the smallest acts of self-care as acts of self-love.** The more you link taking care of yourself and doing things you enjoy to loving yourself, the more you'll see that love grow, and the more you'll find it showing up. Whenever you do what you love to do or take good care of yourself, make a habit of tuning in to feel in your bones how much you deserve this loving treatment. Allow those feelings to grow and be present within you.

   Here's another thing that goes along with this. Begin to see saying yes to what *others* offer to do for you as an act of self-love. So often we tend to be overly self-sufficient, saying "Thanks, I'm good" when people offer to help us out. We women tend to do this most, especially with the men in our lives. Begin to catch yourself turning down offers of help and then reprogram your mind to say, "Yes! Thank you! (*Because I love myself and I deserve*

He paused thoughtfully for a few seconds. "Ahhh, life coach. You help people make a better life? To be happier?"

"Exactly!" I said with a laugh, pleased that he got it. "I love it, and I'm always learning myself."

"We have life coaches here in France. But here I believe we call them seek analysts."

Seek analyst! I loved it! I wasn't entirely sure if that was accurate,

---

help.)" You'll not only feel less frazzled and overwhelmed, you'll also begin to feel more loved—by yourself and others. Receive. It's awesome!

3. **Know what a magnificent miracle you are.** Truly! One of the things that will really crack open your heart to loving yourself fully is to really take the time to ponder what an incredible, amazing miracle you are (we all are). Did you know you are literally made of stardust? Our bodies (and about everything else on earth) are made up of certain elements (carbon, hydrogen, oxygen, etc.), and most of the elements on earth originated from within the center of a star. How amazing is that when you really think about it? We are connected with all things—physically and energetically part of the vastness of the universe.

Our bodies are vehicles for our souls. Just like our bodies, our souls are who we truly are, and they are beautiful miracles here to learn, grow, and serve. You are a soul, residing within an incredible vessel, here to live the human experience.

Everything you've gone through, every victory and every mistake, is part of that experience and was there to guide you in your journey and to your purpose. We are all one with all things. Each of us deserves infinite love, and part of our purpose is to receive this love. We can honor our Source (or higher power) and this life we've been gifted by embracing that purpose through truly loving ourselves.

but I was amused by the idea of the translation, and it certainly worked. Helping people to analyze, discover, and fulfill what they're seeking. I'll take it!

He thoughtfully sipped his Cabernet and then set his glass on the table deliberately. "You really have to love yourself to do that kind of work, no?"

This guy so gets it, I thought. I smiled and immediately answered, "Ohhhh, yeah. I spent the first thirty-two years of my life learning how to love myself, and the last ten helping others to do the same. It's a daily practice."

"Thirty-two years?" he said. "That's a lot of study!" We laughed in unison.

I swear, sometimes the best conversations happen with perfect strangers in random places. After a few more minutes of laughter and small talk, I bid au revoir to the hot Frenchman and spent much of the rest of that day thinking about self-love and how the lack of it in our world just might be our most underrated epidemic.

I believe we are born naturally loving ourselves. Then a panoply of various circumstances and experiences compound over the years, providing fertile ground for our egos to collaborate with those past mistakes and unfavorable experiences to condition us otherwise. It's our job to keep our egos in check and teach them how to use the wisdom gained from past experiences for our own benefit rather than twisting it into (invalid) reasons for beating ourselves up.

Ever see a toddler go through the stage where they discover the meaning and power of the word *no*? For parents, this can be frustrating, annoying, and hilarious all at the same time. But we shouldn't be so quick to squash this behavior. Some call this the terrible twos, but is it really so terrible to learn to passionately state what you don't want and to set boundaries based on pure desire, self-love, and self-assertion? Personally, I think we should all use the word *no* much more often and, at the same time, look to reconnect with the innate self-love and self-worth we naturally had as babies.

When we learn to make truly loving ourselves an integral part of our lives, we live in a way that naturally attracts amazing things.

This way of being shines light on the goodness we deserve and naturally red flags us on situations to avoid.

I can trace so many of the detrimental situations I got myself into when I was younger to a lack of self-love. I'd even blamed others in those scenarios for my own distress, when I was the one truly responsible.

What we tolerate in our lives is a direct reflection of the love we have for ourselves. What's awesome about this is that when we truly start loving ourselves, embracing our worth, and treating ourselves like we are our own best friend, we naturally tolerate much less BS with ease!

In one past relationship with a man I shared a home with, he forbade me to park in the garage because I'd accidentally left it open a handful of times when we'd first moved in. One sunny, peaceful afternoon, I came home from running errands and was literally locked out of my own garage. Instead of expressing my feelings and demanding that my side of the garage be unlocked immediately, I allowed it to continue—for two years.

While I totally understood his initial frustration, his reaction and handling of the situation was extreme and demeaning. He would come down hard on me anytime I would push to park in the safety of the garage instead of on the dark street at night. He would threaten to leave me if I "insisted" on parking in the garage. My garage. So I let it go on. Out of fear. Out of wanting to avoid confrontation. Out of shame. Eventually, the relationship unraveled anyway.

When I think about that time in my life, my heart hurts for the woman I was then. I want to tell her so many things. I want to put my arms around her and pull her to safety from herself. And, holy bananas, do I want her to read this book! Here is what I would say to her if I could.

Oh, dear one. I love you so. You are so amazing. You are worthy of your love and of all the love in the universe, and it's more than you can imagine. You are a precious treasure, a divine creation, and deserve to be treated as such. Walk away from anyone who sees you as anything less than the beautiful, incredible miracle that you are. There are wonderful doors open and waiting, darling (including garage doors!). Doors to freedom, joy, unconditional love, acceptance, and abundant miracles! Walk through them; they were created just for you. Be bold and embrace your greatness. Your most incredible life is waiting, and you are infinitely loved.

Self-love is not easy for everyone. In fact, like so much of what I talk about in this book, it's truly a daily practice—one to be infused in everything you do. For some, the first step to great self-love is just being willing. You may already feel like you love yourself (awesome!), but there is always room for more, trust me. Being willing and open to unconditionally and *actively* love yourself is in itself a great act of self-love. Forgiveness is often the next step, which we're going to talk about shortly.

Finally, I'll wrap up this bit on self-love by encouraging you to love more all around. Across the board. Love all people and all things, even the ones that are hard to love. The more love you give, the more you become love, and the more massive, unlimited love you'll feel for yourself. You are a precious being worthy and deserving of the gift of your beautiful love. Every single day.

HAPPINESS MIND-SET #2: FORGIVENESS

Forgiveness, when correctly embraced and understood, is monumentally powerful and life changing. There are so many misconceptions about what forgiveness is and what it's not. Becoming clear on what forgiveness actually is and how it can free your spirit to soar is the key.

To get started chatting about what forgiveness is, let's start with what it's not. This is stuff that took me a long time to get, but when I did, it changed my life.

Forgiveness is not approval of what the other person did. It doesn't always mean that in some way you agree with or are okay with what went down. And forgiving someone does not automatically mean you must continue to have that person in your immediate circle—or in your life at all. You can completely forgive people and still choose not to have them in your life, temporarily or permanently. Most important, although forgiveness can benefit the other person both energetically and emotionally, it is not for them. *It's for you.*

> " . . . *although forgiveness can benefit the other person both energetically and emotionally, it is not for them. It's for you.*"

Here are a few questions to consider that will help you wrap your heart around these ideas.

○ *How much of your precious energy are you putting into* not *forgiving someone?* Are there higher-quality places in which you could be spending that energy that would improve your life rather than drain it? yeah !

○ *Would you like to be free of negative energy?* Unforgiveness is a form of negative energy. If you are looking to free yourself of—or carry less—negative energy (required in mastering the skill of happiness), you must forgive all and make room for higher vibes. It's also heavy baggage you have to carry around. When you forgive everything, it's like packing light for life.

○ *Can you look deeper to see that what the other person did was based on either love or fear?* If you can't see it, look deeper. It's there in some form. Seeing this will put you in touch with the human side of that person—the side that sometimes makes bad decisions or mistakes—which will make it much easier to forgive.

Now let's talk for a couple of minutes about what forgiveness really *is*. Forgiveness is a sign of great strength. It takes tremendous courage, resolve, and a giving heart. Forgiveness is a great act of self-love.

In order to forgive, you must give. The word *give* is the very heart of the word for*give*ness. It does take energy, and it's not always instant. Even the most naturally forgiving people sometimes need time to process the big stuff before they can completely forgive, so it's totally okay to take your time. Just not too much time. Don't rush yourself, but don't let the issue fester either. Forgiveness and resentment cannot live in the same space.

Consciously make the choice to forgive. Address it and work through it, and you'll feel a shift when you're ready to forgive and let go. Do this regularly with the big stuff and the little stuff, too. All of it. Include the practice of forgiving yourself (yes, you) for anything and everything. You're worthy of this, just like you're worthy of your love.

Free yourself through forgiveness. Let go of all that heaviness and let the light in. Learn to accept apologies you will never receive (that one was huge for me). One step in doing this is to understand that whatever happened wasn't personal, even if the other person is still stuck in a place of making it personal. It's also helpful to allow the other person to be exactly where he or she is, while choosing to believe in your heart that, with an expanded perspective, some part of him or her would understand the hurt they contributed.

Become a natural forgiver by adopting forgiveness as an instinctive mind-set and a go-to choice when things get messed up. Forgive those you feel have wronged you and wish them healing and love.

Forgiveness is the master key that unlocks a great many of the invisible shackles we've put on ourselves.

HAPPINESS MIND-SET #3: COMPASSION

This is such a big one. Compassion is the basis for so much love, kindness, and beauty in the world—and it's certainly a big part of the foundation for forgiveness.

Most of us have a good amount of compassion for others, but what I'd like to say here is that we can all adopt an entirely new level of compassion that is life changing. In fact, if everyone took steps to practice and grow the mind-set of compassion, it would absolutely change the world.

Growing up and all through my twenties, I was compassionate toward others, toward animals always, and even toward fictional characters that experienced epic struggles. But I was not nearly compassionate enough toward those I disagreed with or was in conflict with, which is where compassion is especially powerful. Having compassion for those we don't fully agree with or those we feel have wronged us (or others) in some way brings a new dynamic of love and understanding to any situation. Compassion is light in the darkness, and it fuels change.

Self-compassion was totally absent from my life until my early thirties. When I woke up to the power of self-compassion and realized how hard I'd been on myself for so long, how unforgiving I'd been toward my own sensitive heart, I was immediately driven to create a big change.

I started by looking back at times when I deserved my own compassion, when I deserved to cut myself a break, and sent love, forgiveness, and understanding to my past self, which allowed me to consciously let go of all that heaviness. It was mind-blowing to me how much lighter I felt when I made this shift.

When we understand that we're all doing the best we can with the information, knowledge, and resources we have in each moment, we can find compassion. When we consciously recognize that every single person we meet has his or her own unique struggles, pain, and challenges, we can forgo judgment and view things from a place of understanding, kindness, and empathy.

Compassion, like the other happiness mind-sets in this chapter, is a practice. You don't have to rehash the past to begin living from a place of compassion. Think about people and situations in your life now—people you may have judged, who rub you the wrong way, or toward whom you feel some kind of negative energy. Examine those relationships with a new understanding. Can you acknowledge that we are all connected? That we're all doing the best we can with the knowledge we have? That none of us is perfect, and that's a beautiful thing? See those people who come to mind as miracles and as teachers. Everyone who is living in this lifetime with us has something to teach us. That's an amazing gift if we're willing to receive it, and the way to begin is through compassion.

A simple quote from the Dalai Lama sums up why the practice and mind-set of compassion is so monumentally important: "If you want others to be happy, practice compassion. If you want to be happy, practice compassion."

That pretty much says it all. Whenever you feel yourself reacting toward someone (or yourself) out of anger, frustration, or judgment, work to catch it and see if you can mindfully open your heart and view the situation from a place of compassion before you react further or do any analyzing. With continued effort and practice, this will become natural for you—an amazing new habit—and it will change the way you experience your entire life.

HAPPINESS MIND-SET #4: KINDNESS

Be kind. Surround yourself with truly kind people. It sounds elementary, but I want to emphasize that the energy of kindness is vital to your happiness.

We probably all know a few good, well-meaning people who are not inherently kind. These are people to keep at arm's length. Authentic kindness comes from the soul—from a place of compassion, thoughtfulness, selflessness, and pure love. Seek out people who are innately kind and invite them into your divine circle.

The energy created from giving or receiving genuine loving-kindness not only instantly elevates happiness, it's also good for your health. Science has shown that regular exposure to kindness—both giving and receiving—can actually add years to your life! Not surprising, right?

You know those days when you're just feeling extra kind and super-positive for whatever reason? Spreading random acts of kindness and light, going out of your way to help people or compliment them, and receiving A-game energy in return? Aren't those great days? Imagine what your world would be like if you deliberately created many more of those days or even lived within that vibe a majority of the time. An awesome thought, right? With conscious effort, you can! Imagine what the world would be like if more people were aligned with that mission.

One of the highest levels of positive energy you can cultivate is when you deliberately make the stressed checkout person at the grocery store laugh, compliment a stranger on something you know they worked hard for (a new car, a lovely outfit, a snazzy hairstyle), go out of your way to help someone when they need it, or even just smile electrically at all those in your path. You receive the benefits, and so does everyone around you.

I'm tall, so one of my favorite things to do when I'm out and about is help people reach objects that are high up on shelves at stores. Seriously, it lights me up like I popped a magic pill. Find small ways you can be of service to others or spread good feelings when you're going about your regular days, and work at doing them until they become habit. This is a great way to increase the kindness energy in your life.

At the same time you're looking to step up the kindness factor, look for ways you can dial back on unkindness toward others. None of us wants to admit it, but nearly all of us have sides that we're not so proud of, especially when we feel stressed or our patience is tested. You can be a naturally kind person down to your core and still have a couple of touchy areas that could be improved upon.

When I feel mistreated in some way by a company or service, I have a tendency to direct some of my frustration at customer service people (I know I'm not alone in this). Rotten customer service is a pet peeve of mine, but the customer service reps rarely, if ever, have anything to do with it. I've really been working to be more mindful of this, primarily through tapping into compassion for the overworked reps, and have made significant improvement. Now, I find myself many times joking around with them and telling them their efforts are appreciated—even in the most ridiculous of customer service failures. Much better energy for all.

Be ready to make regular efforts to surround yourself with kind people. It's a permanent work in progress. It takes mindful maintenance of boundaries and willingness to distance yourself from some people who are out of alignment. And when you meet people who radiate kindness, open your heart to learning from them. After all, kindness creates more kindness.

A few years ago on a business trip to New York City, I received a powerful lesson on the energy of kindness from a stranger in an elevator. I'd just checked into my hotel, which was very old, dark, and had a haunted feel. I wasn't thrilled with it, but it was affordable. I clumsily stumbled into the rickety, tiny elevator, lugging all my baggage, and found myself uncomfortably close to a very tall, scruffy-looking man. Hello, awkward moment.

Elevator rides with strangers always seem to be a little weird. You're not sure who's going to push the button, if you should start small talk, or if you should talk at all. I was a little intimidated by this random guy I was squashed next to that afternoon. I'd had a rough day, was worn out from travel, and this dude was huge and looked a bit like he'd just stepped out of a zombie apocalypse movie.

After a long, silent ride up dozens of floors, we reached his stop, and I pulled my wheelie bag out of the way so he could exit. As I did this, a sudden urge to speak to him came to me out of nowhere. "Have a nice day," I blurted out. A well-meaning but mundane statement.

When he stepped out and heard me say those words, he paused, turned toward me, and smiled one of the brightest smiles I'd ever seen. As the elevator doors began to close, he replied, "Have many."

Have many! Many nice days? Yes, please! I will, thanks! His kind response not only made my week, it taught me not to be so quick to be intimidated by people and to always lean toward connection. To let people know I *see* them. A beautiful lesson I received that day from a beautiful man. It was a moment in time I'll never forget.

The Circle of Kindness Exercise

An easy way to start focusing on spending more time with inherently kind people is to take a piece of paper and write down the names of the people in your life—friends, colleagues, neighbors, family, etc. Include all the people you see on a regular or semi-regular basis. Make it a fairly large list. Add people you enjoy being around or would like to see more often, even if you don't know them really well. Then go through the list and circle the ones who are kind and positive and make you feel energized. These are the relationships to focus on growing. It's an eye-opening exercise. Do this on a semiregular basis and it will help you to balance this part of your happiness foundation, as well as make more empowering choices about with whom you spend time.

A while back, I was sitting in the waiting room in the spa at my gym. Several women were in the room with me, including a lovely ninety-four-year-old who glowed with positive energy. A woman who was sitting next to me asked the older one what her secret was for looking and feeling so great at her age. Her answer? "I've always surrounded myself with nice people. That's the secret." Exactly.

HAPPINESS MIND-SET #5: ANYTHING IS POSSIBLE

Anything is possible! Yes, anything. It sounds like a simple statement, and it is. But it doesn't do nearly as much as a statement as it does as a *mind-set*. When you dig deep, you might be shocked to discover the hidden limiting beliefs that are holding you back and lowering the vibes of your life. The anything-is-possible mind-set, when it becomes part of your being, can zap many of those limiting beliefs before they fester and prevent them from warping your groove.

When I was around nineteen, I experienced my very first Cirque du Soleil show. At the time, I thought it was kind of "meh." I remember thinking it was lovely but not really my cup of tea. I just wasn't that moved by it, and I didn't understand all the hype.

Then about four years ago, I went to my first Cirque du Soleil show in twenty years. Remembering my first experience, I wasn't expecting to be tremendously inspired. In fact, I'd expected to be a little bored. I was totally wrong; I was completely astonished by it! The ridiculously talented performers and the amazing, graceful, seemingly impossible things they were able to do blew me away. It really was incredible, and for the first time, I understood why they get so much well-deserved acclaim.

In the days after seeing that show, I couldn't shake my curiosity about the contrast between the first time I'd seen the performance and this time. Why was I so uninspired the first time and completely amazed by it all these years later? Then the answer came, and it made absolute sense. I wasn't that awed by it the first time because as a very young woman, I didn't have nearly the collection of limiting beliefs that I have now! So nothing they were doing then seemed all that impossible or unbelievable to me at the time. However, this last time, I had twenty extra years' worth of limiting beliefs about things not being possible or being hard to do, and it made everything they were doing seem absolutely incredible. My brain was primed to have some of those negative, limiting beliefs totally challenged!

After this realization, I wanted to shift to an anything-is-possible way of thinking so I could begin to see my life and the world the way I saw that first Cirque du Soleil show. Like anything is 100 percent possible, especially if we're willing to be surprised! It made no sense to go into anything else thinking there was a 30, 50, or 70 percent chance of making it work, which is exactly how I'd been operating—always with some doubt present to suck energy from the effort.

I wanted to start approaching life believing that there's a 100 percent chance things can go my way every time. Not that they always will, but *believing* it's always possible—and *probable*—is key not only to raising the vibration of every situation but also to creating a more positive experience overall, no matter the outcome. An absolute YES attitude. Plus, it's a pretty fun way to go about your days, truly believing anything is possible and allowing yourself to just be in awe of the universe and its miracles coming your way all the time.

For inspiration, I looked for people I admire who seem to embody the *anything-is-possible mind-set*. Oprah, check. Long-distance swimmer Diana Nyad, check. Richard Branson, oh, hell yeah! Check. They've all taken tremendous risks to be where they are. They went after their dreams full force, believing they could absolutely happen even when the journey didn't go exactly as planned. If Richard Branson had listened to all the doubters and naysayers when he started Virgin Galactic, or if he'd quit after devastating setbacks, we would not be well on our way to achieving commercial space flight and several other amazing advances. Can you imagine the doors he's going to open for the world?

When I first started to create this change in my way of thinking, I would look to catch myself anytime I was tempted to slip into an "it's all over," "the chances are slim," or "it's just not going to happen" thought pattern and shift to "it's not over yet!" and "it's definitely possible!" instead. After a while, this effort changed the way my mind sees every situation.

> *"Miracles are everywhere when we look, and especially when we allow them to be. Part of allowing them to be is <u>believing</u> in them in the first place."*

I've always been very optimistic. But even the most optimistic people can get saddled with limiting beliefs. Approaching life and everything you do with an ever-present knowing in your heart that *anything is possible* creates incredible momentum. And it changes the way you experience your life, creating more peace, joy, and vision in all you do.

ANYTHING is possible. Anything. Miracles are everywhere when we look and, especially, when we allow them to be. Part of allowing them to be is *believing* in them in the first place.

In the final section of this chapter, I'm going to share some techniques that really work to create these mind-set shifts and significant changes we can make to regain power over our thoughts, because our thoughts create our lives. Taking charge of them can be like herding cats, but once you practice and become great at it (and you will), your life will be forever changed.

Say it out loud: ANYTHING IS POSSIBLE.

Believe it. Feels great, doesn't it?

THE HAPPINESS SUPER-SHIFT: THOUGHT MANAGEMENT

"What do I think about when I strike out? I think about hitting home runs."
—Babe Ruth

If you've done any kind of personal development or spiritual work prior to picking up this book, you're already aware how important our thoughts are in shaping our lives. You may have heard the saying "Thoughts become things," and if you haven't, well, it's absolutely true. Thoughts are not just important; they are the entire foundation of our lives and how we live and encounter it.

Our thoughts are responsible for every choice we make, everything we create or destroy, and, yes, they're responsible for the amount of happiness we experience. If you do just one thing after reading this book, commit yourself to increasing awareness of your thoughts and then changing the ones that need it. Thought awareness and management, or mindfulness, is the true key to owning your power over your thoughts and mind-sets and making them work for you to support your happiest life, rather than work against you.

Some thoughts are so obvious, they're pretty easy to catch and control, especially negative self-talk related to a current situation, like "I'm totally going to mess this interview up!" We all have negative self-talk now and then. I'm always working to stay on top of this and have created a huge positive shift. Now it's rare, but when I do catch it, I turn the thoughts into loving, supportive ones toward myself, and it instantly makes everything so much better! Negative self-talk is super-damaging, unloving, and unnecessary, so this is the perfect place to begin creating a shift.

Beneath the more obvious, everyday negative thoughts, there are some that are so ingrained that we have to dig a little deeper to sweep them out, like dust bunnies in the back of our closets. We may not even realize they're there until we pull some stuff back and look closer. They're thoughts we've carried with us for years—"thought baggage" is a good way to describe them—and we want to lose these once and for all so we can replace them with awesome, supportive thoughts and affirmations.

Evergreen negative thoughts we've carried for a long time could include "I'm just not good at math" (oh, I was so guilty of that one for so long!), or "I had a difficult childhood" (why keep affirming this?), or *anything* that begins with "I hate . . . " or resembles an unnecessary complaint. Now, I'm a believer that some complaints, when constructive and respectful, are a necessary part of our self-care, so there is no need to ban all complaining. But we all know the difference between complaints that serve a purpose and ones that do nothing but create negative vibes.

The Laboratory of Neuro Imaging at the University of Southern California states that the number of thoughts the average person thinks per day is 70,000. Other estimates say it can range between 12,000 and 50,000. After a quick self-assessment, I came up with an average of about 17,500 for me. Wow! That's a boatload of thoughts! Can you imagine the impact on our lives when a large chunk of those thoughts are negative? How that might be affecting us physically and emotionally?

Let's have a moment of realness right now. For the purpose of perspective, let's say we have 20,000 thoughts per day. Take a moment and ask yourself what percentage of your thoughts lately could be considered negative or unsupportive. Close your eyes and think about this for a minute and let an honest answer come from your inner voice. Perhaps 30 percent? 50 percent? 70 percent? Then, using the 20,000 number as a total, do the math to figure out how many negative thoughts you're having each day. For many people, this will be at least 50 percent on average, which is 10,000 negative thoughts per day. No matter your number, there is room to do some positive work in this area. It's time to take the reins and seize control of your thoughts once and for all to empower your best life.

Each thought we have is energy. The incredible news here is that the frequency and light of that energy is *our choice*. We have more power than we realize to make the great majority of the thoughts we think positive, supportive, and healthy. It just takes mindful effort to create a profound shift.

Later on, we'll dive into an entire chapter on how mindfully managing your first thoughts of the day can change your life. We'll go even deeper on this topic, because I believe learning to change our thoughts is the path to changing our world. When I really got a handle on this, it was like I was completely in charge of my life for the first time ever! The change was *that* huge. We don't realize how much our rambling, stray thoughts control us until we take control of them. Like all the practices and mind-sets I'm sharing in this book, it takes weeks or even months of dedication and practice to become good at it, but once you do, the positive change is miraculous.

Mindful Practice: Talk to Your Thoughts

It may sound a little nuts, but believe it or not, actively talking to your thoughts—even having conversations with them in your mind—can be a super-effective way to consciously take control and create immediate change when you catch yourself in a pattern

Small Shifts to Make Today

To simplify getting started, here are the top three small shifts you can make that get big results.

- **Focus on what you want to attract.** In most situations, especially those that involve fear, we tend to focus on what we don't want instead of what we do want. When you catch yourself thinking about the outcome you don't want (i.e., thoughts that begin with "I don't want . . . " or "I hope this doesn't. . . ," etc.), pause and reverse them to thoughts that begin with "I'd like to see . . . " and "The outcome I'd like is. . . ." You'll be amazed by how this will change your energy, experience, and even the outcome.

- **Unfriend your inner critic.** Kick that negative naysayer to the curb. When you begin beating yourself up in your mind (or out loud) for anything, squash that negative self-talk! This doesn't mean you should avoid personal responsibility for mistakes, but it does mean you should be kinder to yourself and ban all useless negative language about your beautiful self. You deserve kindness, always. Once you practice eliminating this, it will make a huge difference in how you feel overall. You'll just be . . . a little lighter.

- **When you notice yourself in a stressful or bluesy place, ask yourself questions about the way you're thinking in those moments.** A great one I keep in my pocket is "Is the way I'm thinking right now encouraging or discouraging?" That question always produces a clarifying answer and is like a turbo boost for an immediate change in vibration. You can also try asking, "Is there another way I can look at this that might be more supportive?

of negative thinking. With this surprisingly effective (and kind of fun, once you get used to it) technique, you can empower yourself to create small shifts in your thinking by recognizing negative thoughts and actually conversing with them. Sometimes, I even speak to my thoughts out loud (with nobody else around, of course, or they'd probably be very concerned).

To begin, start to deliberately raise awareness of your thoughts on a consistent basis. When you notice a negative, unwanted, or draining thought, interrupt it and start a conversation with it from the positive, loving being that you are within. For example, if you catch yourself thinking "I'm afraid I'm going to mess up my job interview today," acknowledge the thought and say something along the lines of "Thanks for showing up today, negative thought, but you're not invited to this party. I'm going to rock this interview and they're going to be so happy they took the time to meet with me!"

It may feel weird at first, but seriously, this works. You can use this anytime you notice negative thoughts or negative self-talk (jump in and defend yourself) or catch yourself thinking about things you know are not serving you at that moment (such as negative experiences from the past). This will help retrain your mind by interrupting negative thoughts and replacing them with higher-quality ones. After you do this for a while, you'll feel a shift in your entire way of thinking. You'll notice fewer negative thoughts and many more positive, joyful thought patterns. Your energy and the way you feel overall will be lighter.

Now I'm not saying to become all Pollyannaish. Of course, there is a purpose for some of the hurtful thoughts that creep in from time to time, and those sometimes need to be examined and resolved so we can let go and move forward. And it's not to say we have to become perfect at being all positive all the time. That's just not human. The idea is to greatly reduce our number of negative thoughts and replace them with healthy, uplifting, empowering thoughts. This is life changing.

When I started consciously creating these interruptions and shifts in my thoughts a few years ago, I noticed instant changes in my entire demeanor. I can remember one instance where I was standing in my massively messy kitchen, thinking "I can't believe I'm letting the kitchen get this gross. I'm the worst housekeeper. What's wrong with me?" SO not productive. I caught this and said back to the thought, "Sorry, but you're not contributing here. I've been very busy with wonderful things lately and the kitchen hasn't been a priority. I'll get to it soon enough." Instantly, I went from feeling like crap about the kitchen to seeing not having cleaned it yet as a choice to use that energy where it was needed at the time to support my happiness. I felt lighter and more peaceful right away. Right on!

I have to admit, I've also been known to swear at my negative thoughts now and then when inspired. An f-bomb here and there in the right context can be very empowering. Just saying.

Getting Started

To get accustomed to the concept of conversing with your thoughts, try taking a sheet of paper or your journal and list a few of the thoughts you've had lately that could have been changed to better serve your happiness. Next to them, list the thoughts that could replace them and make them empowering. This will help you to get clear on how to converse with those pesky negative thoughts when they pop in. Then you can start doing this in your mind, and you'll notice immediate results. And I'm talking immediate. Have fun with it. Stick with it. This will support you for a long time to become another effective tool in your Operation Happiness toolkit.

I encourage you to go deep in living and *becoming* the mind-sets I've covered in this chapter. Work at it. You will see immediate changes, but it will take time and mindful dedication to create lasting results that will form the fundamental parts of your happiness foundation. (There are excellent books available on each one. See the Suggested Reading section on page 245.) It's not about being perfect, it's about elevating and expanding each of these mind-sets in your heart, consciousness, and life. Choose them over and over, practice them, and deliberately operate from them until they become part of your DNA. It will change everything.

Proverbs 3:13

"Happy is the man that findeth Wisdom, and the man that getteth understanding.

"Cast not your pearls before swine."
                    Proverbs
34. Surely he scorneth the scorners: but he giveth grace unto the lowly.

35. The wise shall inherit (glory): but shame shall be the promotion of fools.   9/24/2017 @
                                        1205 am

CHAPTER 3

Happiness in Hard Times: Creating the Light within Darkness

Of all the chapters in this book, this one, for me personally, was the most challenging to write. To reach the depths of service I truly want to offer you, I had to purposefully go back to some of the most difficult times in my life, to remember and feel some of the feelings of being there, so I could fully embrace what some of you may be experiencing right now, or will be when you come back to this chapter in need of support. In this chapter, I'll share some very personal things with you and some of the most powerful practices and mind-sets that got me through the roughest seas I could ever have imagined.

Sometimes, life doesn't just throw you lemons, it throws you grenades. Personal struggle, transition, illness, loss of loved ones—these are all unavoidable events that every single one of us will experience at some point on our journey. This fact can't be ignored (as nice as it is to not think about it). Happy people aren't exempt from hard times; they're just armed with the foundation, outlook, and effective tools to help them navigate, survive, and heal successfully, as well as create the best possible outcomes.

It always amazes me when friends or family say to me, "What do you mean you're having a hard week? Aren't you supposed to be the happiness expert?" It truly cracks me up. I wonder if they think I'm some kind of wind-up joy robot. (Far from it!) But I have learned some of the most supportive ways to deal with the unexpected lemons and grenades that life can throw at us.

Here, I'll be offering some insight and powerful tools that will be useful to you in everyday challenges, as well as hugely supportive in getting through life's most catastrophic events and transitions. They have all been immensely helpful to me in my own personal journey. Some I've discovered through research, some I've learned through great teachers, and some I've come to know through my own experience.

Think of this chapter as its own little book within a book. You can read it now, as well as come back to it when you feel you need loving support and guidance.

To me, a book about creating a happy life without a serious conversation about ways to get through very difficult times is like a car without windshield wipers. Everything's great until it rains, and then what? Part of building a foundation for sustainable happiness involves preparing to weather the most challenging times with as much peace, light, and inner fitness as possible. The way to do this is to gain skills that help us create supportive, go-to responses for emotional pain and tools to help us find the strength to take baby steps toward healing that lift us up, help us process, and empower us through our journey. Part of changing our view about happiness is embracing the idea that there are always encouraging tools and resources to reach for in any life situation if we're willing to take action.

MY RETURN FROM ROCK BOTTOM

When I went through my long period of illness in 2008, the transformational journey it sent me on not only changed my life into one of sustainable happiness, it also aptly prepared me for a monumental dark storm that was headed right for me. Over the next two years following my recovery, two of my dearest childhood friends passed away suddenly—one through suicide, one through addiction— terrible tragedies that left me heartbroken and also prompted me to examine a few realities in my own life. My priorities had changed big time since becoming happier, and they changed even further with the loss of my friends. I didn't know it at the time, but a foundation had been laid that would get me through the darkest time of my life.

In early 2012, I was faced with the heart-wrenching end of my ten-year marriage. It ran me down like a stampede of elephants, leaving me desperately lost, reeling, and shattered with bone-crushing grief. I'd been through plenty of losses, failures, and broken hearts in my life up until that point, but nothing even closely resembled the devastation that had just enveloped me like a tidal wave.

I realized during that time that, although I'd been through some serious stuff in my life, until then, I'd never really experienced true, soul-twisting grief in all its devastating and transformational wonder. Suddenly, I was facing the rest of my life without the person I'd planned to spend it with.

Many resources and practices got me through my fog of pain during the couple of years that followed. Many of them I've covered already in previous chapters, and I'll share several more of them with you here. One of the biggest sources of help was the deep belief in my soul that all the destruction and explosive heartache had the potential to be the greatest growth opportunity and biggest transformational journey of my life. I had to believe this to keep breathing. Turns out I was right.

I would survive starting over. I would forgive and learn from my mistakes. I would make it through rebuilding, and I would thrive. Sometimes pulling your life together in the best possible way begins with taking it all apart.

While picking up the pieces of my world, I became intensely

focused on looking for lessons and for grace. They truly are every-where . . . if you look. Honestly, some days the pain was so great I couldn't possibly imagine anything good coming out of it. Grief can be deceiving that way. But in early 2014, as I came out of my cloud of hurt and looked at what the concrete foundation of my own cul-tivated strength, learned happiness skills, and mindful determination to heal had created, I was astonished and immensely proud.

> *"While picking up the pieces of my world, I became intensely focused on looking for lessons and for grace. They truly are everywhere . . . if you look."*

Somehow, while in that fog, I'd gone on an amazing, messy, rocky adventure of rebuilding, expanding, renewing, and even being a bit reckless. I'd finally landed on my feet wiser, stronger, and with more love and compassion for myself and others than ever before. It wasn't easy, but it was worth the fight.

In a nutshell, the previous couple of years had consisted of tons of yoga; zillions of tears; daily prayer (which sometimes involved pleading); a ridiculously unrealistic—but passionate—relationship with a super-charismatic, intelligent guy who was twelve years younger; letting go of a home that I once thought was my dream house; downsizing and getting rid of 70 percent of everything I owned; buying a small home on a plot of land in Los Angeles on which I started an urban farm; traveling to Hawaii, the Bahamas, London, Paris, and Bucharest; a relationship with a sweetheart of a guy who was in no place to be in a relationship (neither was I, for that matter—a reminder that *we attract what we are*); and, finally, taking a summer off from it all to be alone and just breathe. What a hell of a ride!

When all that was behind me, I began to seriously think about writing a book again. Prior to the end of my marriage, I'd been putting notes and plans together for a book on happiness and even had one outlined. But wow, everything had changed so much since then, and it was all on an entirely new level now. There was so much more valuable information to share! I scrapped all my old notes and started fresh with more clarity than I'd ever had.

There were times back in the midst of the storm when I felt like maybe I was the last person on the planet who should write a book on happiness. But when I stepped out of the ashes into my new life after everything I'd been through and learned in the past decade, I realized not only that I was exactly the person to write this book but also that I *must* write it.

I could now clearly see that the happiness foundation I'd built prior to the storm sustained me through even the darkest days. When truly the last thing I wanted to do was get out of bed, my belief that our lives are ultimately shaped by the way we start our mornings would give me the tiny spark I needed to get myself up, get out of my sweatpants, and put one foot in front of the other. I could also see that my learned nature to always seek things that lift me up, even the smallest things, had helped me to move forward and discover some new, incredibly powerful practices for my happiness toolbox.

IMPORTANT ADDITIONS TO YOUR HAPPINESS TOOLBOX

In addition to all the other skills, mind-sets, and tools I share in this book, I want to share some specific ones with you that helped me to get through difficult times. These are skills and ideas to help navigate choppy waters of all kinds and bring on the healing.

Feel Your Feelings

Do all you can to heal and feel better, but try not to do things too often for the sole purpose of numbing your pain. When my marriage ended and I found myself alone for the first time in nearly twelve years, I went for massages and to yoga classes every chance I could get. But I looked at them as healthful opportunities to let emotions flow rather than bury them. If you could have seen all the times tears would fall onto my yoga mat during the downward-facing dog pose, you'd be like, "OMG, you poor thing!" But the truth is, yoga mat tears were some of the most freeing and empowering.

That's not to say *never* do anything with the sole purpose of numbing your pain. Sometimes you need a break. Just make wise choices that will ultimately support you rather than destructive ones that will hinder your growth and healing.

I jumped on more planes than I can even remember while going through my divorce, thanks to banked airline miles and a good friend who happens to be a flight attendant. I love to travel and find it hugely healing and educational at the same time. All the travel helped to distract me at times from the pain of my loss but also helped me to process it and see the beautiful possibility of the new life I was stepping into.

While I know not everyone can jump on a bunch of planes, this was a part of my path that helped me to constructively move forward. Different things work for different people; the key is to find things that are doable for you and bring even the tiniest spark of light into your heart in the midst of a storm, and then *deliberately* bring them into your space as often as possible. It could indeed be a trip somewhere, but it could also be hiking in the mountains, losing yourself in beautiful books, volunteering for a cause you believe in, going to watch movies solo, planting a garden, or spending lots of time with dear friends—whatever speaks to your soul. The experiences you'll receive through taking radical action will help you feel alive again.

On a solo trip to Hawaii, I can remember swimming out into the ocean and getting whacked with a sudden, aching wave of emotion that comes along with grief. Grief is like that. One minute you're doing okay, and the next, you feel like someone just slugged you in the stomach. (This is totally normal, by the way.)

I stopped and began to tread water, looking back at the beach. I decided to just let the tears flow. Knowing they were blending seamlessly into the sea was a deep comfort. I said to myself out loud, "You're going to be better than okay, I promise." After a couple of minutes of treading and sobbing, I felt surprisingly lighter. Better. I swam back to shore with renewed energy, feeling reconnected to purpose and healing (and ready for a mai tai). It was a reminder to never underestimate the power of a good cry. Seriously. It's part of a happy life.

Give It 90 Seconds

One of the most fascinating and helpful pieces of information I came across when researching healing tools was from neuroscientist and author Dr. Jill Bolte Taylor, PhD. (I'm a huge fan of her amazing work.) She says when a person has a thought that brings a strong emotional response (such as the moment I experienced while swimming in Hawaii), a ninety-second chemical process happens in the body, after which it flushes out. If the strongest waves of emotion remain after the ninety seconds, it's because we've chosen to allow them to continue. Basically, it's like hitting a "replay" button. We can consciously choose to move back into the present and allow waves of anger, grief, and other strong emotions to dissolve, and our body will support us by essentially switching gears. Amazing stuff, right?

In her book *My Stroke of Insight*, Dr. Taylor shares that when you're hit with thoughts that trigger big waves of emotion, you can choose to feel and breathe through them for around ninety seconds and then consciously choose to return to the present moment, move forward, and allow the natural release to occur within your brain and body. Do this repeatedly when going through difficult times, and it will become one of your rock-solid, go-to emotional fitness tools. It did for me.

Try Ho'oponopono

There are many layers to Ho'oponopono, the ancient Hawaiian practice of forgiveness, reconciliation, and problem solving. I consider myself a dedicated student rather than a teacher, but I'd like to introduce you to it and share with you how it has helped me greatly. It's truly one of the most profound and effective spiritual practices I've ever come across for emotional healing and clearing.

Ho'oponopono is incredibly powerful and simple, and it's a practice that has completely transformed the way I handle any painful conflict in my life. I first learned of it while writing an article on forgiveness a few years back. At first I was like, "Ho-O-WHAT?" But being a person who is passionate about the power of forgiveness and feels deeply connected to the islands of Hawaii and their history, I was immediately intrigued and wanted to learn more.

The art of Ho'oponopono began in ancient Hawaiian culture as a ritual and spiritual practice that would help families work through conflict, especially when a family member was sick, as it was believed that a person's mistakes were the root of illness (probably not far off in some cases even today, right?). It begins with a prayer, then acknowledging and working through the problem, reflection, repentance, and forgiveness. Today, it has evolved into a widely known and loved way of resolving conflict, practicing forgiveness, taking responsibility, changing the vibrations of a situation, and clearing hearts.

In the 1970s, healer Morrnah Nalamaku Simeona, a Hawaiian *kahuna lapa'au* (healing priest), adapted Ho'oponopono in a way that it could be practiced solo rather than just with a family or group. Dr. Ihaleakala Hew Len, PhD, a former student of Simeona, continues to teach and expand on Simeona's modernized principles of Ho'oponopono today, as does author and seminar leader Mabel Katz, whose expert teachings on Ho'oponopono have been a helpful guide for me.

Part of more modern Ho'oponopono involves a powerful and

simple healing prayer, or mantra. Every time a person, conflict, or situation that you're struggling with comes into your mind, mentally repeat over and over again, "Thank you," or "I love you," or run together the four phrases:

"I'm sorry. Please forgive me. Thank you. I love you."

Repetition of this magical, cleansing mantra of healing words can lift dark clouds within minutes, help to transform and even erase negative memories, and change the vibrations you're feeling around the whole situation. It's about taking complete responsibility, forgiveness, love, clearing, and gratitude. Since memories are playing in our minds all the time, it's helpful to repeat the mantra often. I sometimes do this for a few minutes straight, almost like a meditation, and sometimes, I just say it one time or a few times together throughout the day. You can even say the phrases when you're feeling good for prevention and to maintain the healing flow. Feel the energies flow through your mind and body and know the energies are being sent directly to the other person.

When you say the words *I'm sorry* and *Please forgive me*, you're taking responsibility for your part in a situation, no matter how small you feel your part may be and no matter who you feel is at fault. Because the truth is, you really don't know yet what actually caused a situation or what the purpose is meant to be. Saying you're sorry for any hurt caused by the situation (compassion), taking personal responsibility without guilt, and finding compassion is amazingly freeing and healing. This is also about releasing attachment to your feelings of being wronged, forgiving yourself, telling a new story, knowing you are responsible for your own feelings and views, and clearing space in your heart.

When you say *Thank you* and *I love you*, you're expressing gratitude for the person or people involved, for the lessons you've learned, for their understanding, and for the opportunity to grow. You're thanking yourself for being willing to take responsibility for your healing and to find forgiveness and embody love. You're expressing thanks for the guidance you're receiving. Then you're connecting to the energy of unconditional love.

With all this, you're creating and feeling the vibration of authentic pure love, forgiveness, clarity, and healing within your heart, and you're surrounding the entire situation with love and light. Through this practice, you will actually feel a shift in your physical body. Your heart will feel lighter and your mind more at peace. It truly is miraculous.

For me personally, the concept I mentioned earlier of letting our emotions flow and honoring them for ninety seconds and the practice of Ho'oponopono went together beautifully during the darkest times. When waves of heartache would flood my body, I would breathe and repeat the mantra, focusing on the present until the distress melted into peace and clarity.

Ho'oponopono has played a huge part not just in my healing, but in many areas of my life. It's beautifully powerful. Many teachers and students have grown and benefited from its powerful yet easy-to-understand process. If you'd like to go deeper, I've listed some resources on page 245.

Don't Minimize or Compare Your Suffering

This is a big one, and it's a destructive trap that takes conscious effort to avoid. Have you ever heard yourself saying anything that resembles "Well, what I'm going through pales in comparison to what so-and-so is going through" or "There are people much worse off than I am, so I should feel grateful . . ."? This tends to squash our legitimate grief and pain, resulting in guilt and anxiety for feeling the way we do. Who needs more junk to feel when we're already going through a hard enough time?

The truth is, if you look for them, there will always be people who are going through things to which our hard times seem to pale in comparison. There will always be somebody who seems to have it worse. It's important to remember that you are not them, and they are not you. You can still acknowledge the suffering of others and feel great compassion for them, but stay away from comparisons. They're hurtful, irrelevant, and can detract from healing. There is something to be said about gaining valuable perspective from what others have been through and how they've handled it, but this is different from minimizing our own suffering by comparison.

What you're going through at any given time in your life is your journey, and your suffering and grief are valid and real. Give yourself permission to feel the way you do, to seek out resources that will help you, and to filter out anything you just don't have the bandwidth for, which includes taking on and comparing your feelings to the suffering of others.

Realize Hope Is Overrated

I know hope has a great reputation for being a beautiful thing, and it can be, but the truth is that it can also be damaging. Hoping to change what we can't control can block healing and so can repeatedly wishing we could go back or wishing things were different.

When I finally consciously let go of any hope that my husband would have a change of heart about wanting to move on, I could direct that emotional effort toward healing and moving on myself. It was a great lesson in surrender and taking back my own power. Hope in the wrong situations can be a form of misdirected energy.

To truly be free of some things, you must be *willing* to let go of them. Hope can sometimes be one of those things. When you're ready, draw a line in the sand and make room in your heart to move forward, be free, and let the light in.

Listen to Others, But Be Selective

People have a hard time figuring out what to say when someone they know has been blindsided by a major life change. Whether it's divorce, death of a loved one, job loss, illness, or something else big, well-meaning people can sometimes overstep with their advice and opinions. Be open to receiving all the love and support they're offering, but trust your heart, take plenty of time to think about any big decisions that need to be made (especially financial ones), and be selective about what you listen to.

Years ago, when I left my management job in the corporate world and was thinking about starting my own company, many people told me how so many small businesses fail and that I should really consider sticking with a secure job. It was a hard time for me emotionally. I'd left that job because staying there in a negative environment became more painful than the idea of being unemployed. All the advice I received about whether or not to start my own business definitely caused me to hesitate a bit and left me somewhat fearful. Today, I'm so grateful I took the risk and went out on my own. I wouldn't be doing what I do today if it wasn't for the fact that all those years ago I was willing to trust and go for it.

Also, know that sometimes when you share everything you're going through with others, even when they love you and have the best of intentions, they can be judgmental about your feelings and choices because they won't fully understand your experience unless they've been through an extremely similar one. When this happens, recognize it for what it is and don't let it cause you to question yourself. Just because someone helps you through a situation, it does not give that person the right to judge you about it.

Throw a Fit

Allow yourself to throw a fit. A real one. A total, complete mess of a stomping, angry, ridiculous fit that would make any two-year-old envious. Tantrums can be freeing, healthy, and healing. Forget trying to be stoic or graceful for a while. Sometimes, the most graceful way to handle something is to be decidedly *un*graceful. To break down, sob, stumble, scream, be pissed off, and say exactly what's on your mind. Through honoring your truth, true grace rises, even out of a tantrum.

"Sometimes, the most graceful way to handle something is to be decidedly <u>ungraceful</u>."

When my husband and I split, I threw at least a fit a day for weeks, and then several a month for quite a while. It actually felt good. If I'd let things bottle up, I'd have exploded like a volcano. Sometimes, I'd finish a huge tantrum and find myself laughing at how crazy and foolish it seemed, yet feel incredibly powerful at the same time. Some unfortunate pillows took many beatings. I'd finish with a "Hell yeah! I've got this and I *will* get through it!"

When letting emotions flow without restraint, sometimes we can gain valuable insight that we wouldn't have been clear on when keeping a lid on things. I can remember a few times when I would spontaneously scream something out loud and then think to myself, "I didn't know I even felt that way, but that makes sense!"

It's okay to feel angry, to feel compassion for yourself for what you're going through, and to ask why. If you feel like you need to do these things while stomping your feet, yelling, and beating up a pillow, know that this is perfectly okay and just go for it.

Put Together a Pro Team

When something monumental happens in your life, you'll likely need professional help from someone who is paid to offer you the kind of support and resources you need. Only you will truly know what you need, and your friends and family can only help so much. My team was made up of a fantastic doctor, a coach, a nutritionist, a massage therapist, a housekeeper, a financial advisor, and a great marriage and family therapist who specialized in grief. I didn't necessarily turn to all of them at once, but interchangeably and as needed (and as budget would allow).

One thing I learned from lining up my amazing team of helpful professionals was that I love having them! Even after my life came back together in miraculous ways, I've kept them all on speed dial.

Having professional help, care, and advice where you need it is not a luxury; it's a vital part of good self-care.

Expect the Unexpected

When you go through a major loss or transition in your life, it changes everything: The way you see yourself and your life changes profoundly. The way you see the world changes. Opinions about random things like world affairs and politics that were once deep-seated may change. You may even shock yourself. Collateral changes you'd never expect begin to take place. You tolerate less but have more compassion than ever. Your capacity for BS is not what it used to be. You may even feel like you've become a completely different person—stronger, wiser, softer, and with a few permanent scars. To me, scars, inside or out, are not bad. I see them as signs of a full life.

Last year, I went through this really weird thing for a couple of weeks where I felt intuitively that something was out of whack in my life. I spent a few days analyzing myself and turning inward for the answer, but nothing came. It felt as if something inside me was constantly tugging at my shirt, trying to get my attention.

Finally one evening, I was wandering around my house thinking, examining furniture, touching objects, and reflecting on memories from a past life. I stopped in my dimly lit hallway to look at the photos on the wall. I'd seen them all hundreds of times before, but in that moment, a black-and-white photo of me holding my baby niece gave me the answer I'd been seeking.

I stood staring at the photo, astounded by the message I'd just received. Although the photo had been taken five years earlier, I remembered the day so clearly. We were at the zoo, and my husband (at the time), a talented photographer, snapped a beautiful candid shot of me holding the little one up to see the meerkat exhibit. It became one of my favorite photos of all time. Now, looking at it, I saw something amazing. *I needed to mourn the woman in that photo.* That happy, peaceful woman who had no idea what was coming at the time. I needed to send her love, tell her she did the best she could . . . and let her go.

Since the end of my marriage, I'd mourned so many things. The deep love we'd shared, my old life, the life we'd planned together. I never expected that when I was through all that, I would also need to mourn the person I used to be. When I realized this, it all made perfect sense. Now that my life was basically back together and I was feeling great, this was the final step in moving forward and fully accepting who I am today. I loved who I was then, but I really love who I am now!

That night, I lit a candle, sat on my couch, and repeated the Ho'oponopono prayer many times. Only this time, I was not picturing my ex. I was picturing the old me. *I'm sorry. Please forgive me. Thank you. I love you.* When I woke up the next morning, the unsettled feeling that had been with me for weeks had vanished.

When it comes to unexpected changes that take place after a major life event, I can tell you that not all of them are easy, but they're all necessary gifts for moving forward. Stay open and accepting of what comes your way. Take a step back from each change as it happens to look for the light. It's there.

One thing that will very likely happen (and if you've been through a huge loss or change before, you know exactly what I mean here) is that when you take a dramatically new path, not everyone you love comes with you on your journey. In the way that trees shed leaves and drop fruit when the seasons change, people will disappear from our lives when our own seasons change.

Some people won't understand your pain or approve of your choices. Some will be thoroughly rude and insensitive. Some won't understand or approve of the new you. You'll discover that some of the people in your life liked the old you better. The more-tolerant you. The one who didn't desire the depth and support from relationships that you look for now.

You may have to make the hard decision to distance yourself

from some who have become draining or toxic. Send them love, gratitude, and forgiveness. Then wish them peace and let them go to make room for new people who share your vibe and bring fresh new energy to your life.

You'll find that the people who truly love you will stick by you through even the most unimaginable hardship, no matter how long it takes you to climb out of it (and don't let anyone tell you to rush or to "get over it already"). Sometimes, they're even the ones holding the rope as you climb.

The people who are still standing after the storm will become diamonds in your life. Let them fall in love all over again with the reborn, reimagined, amazing new you.

This doesn't mean that all the relationships that fall away will be gone for good. Some just need a rest and will heal and blossom again when they're meant to circle back. It's all just a part of the natural process of growth.

Be open and hold on. Know that some of the paramount, most extraordinary things in life result from the unexpected.

Notice Supportive Signs

I've learned that there are always supportive signs to be received if we're open to spotting them. Call them grace, serendipity, divine guidance . . . all are appropriate. One of the truly amazing things about life is all the little events that make nothing seem random. Notice them and embrace them in any way that feels good to you.

A few days after my husband moved out, I was at one of the lowest points of my life. I looked like death and felt like it, too. I knew my body needed extra nutrition, and I needed to stay hydrated. Determined to do all I could to stay physically well, I forced myself to get in the car and head to a little vegan café down the road for a green juice. I approached the counter and asked the charmingly earthy server if they had a juice option made with kale, ginger, and lemon. She replied, "Absolutely! It's called the Learn to Let Go." My eyes grew wide and I burst out laughing. She probably thought I was a crazy person. It was the first time I'd laughed in weeks, and I felt a welcome wave of loving support from the universe flow though me. I ordered two of the magic drinks, and as I headed back to my car I whispered, "Thanks. Got that."

Look Back for Good Reason

Although looking back on the past is sometimes unproductive, reflecting on what you've been through can bring beautiful clarity and enlightenment at times. It's perfectly okay, necessary in fact, to stand on top of the greatest mountains you've climbed with the wind in your hair and the sun on your face to look down on all you've conquered. To say "I did it." It's part of spreading your wings and letting everything you've learned become part of your DNA. And it's a crucial, magical part of letting go and moving forward into your next season.

One thing I was clear on after coming out of my own dark times was that without the happiness foundation I'd built, and so many of the ideas and tools I'm sharing in this book, those times would have been much darker.

I also realized that through it all, even on the most difficult days, I never lost the deep sense that underneath all the heaviness bearing down on me was my true nature of happiness; I could see that happiness can be found in the space between our most challenging moments if we're willing to look (and train our minds to do so). We can allow that nature to support us, guide us, and be the light at the end of even the longest tunnels. This is the true meaning of lasting, sustainable happiness. At the same time, we must also know that our darkest times will never define or defeat our happiness.

Allowing ourselves to be guided through life by love and our true nature of happiness takes mindful practice, and it's an ongoing effort. But if we step onto this amazing path and don't deviate, it's the one path that will always be illuminated, no matter the obstacles that appear.

I know I'll have times down the road when I'll need to circle back to the conversation here in this chapter and remind myself of all the power we have over the way we navigate the circumstances presented to us. To remember the ninety seconds of breathing, the prayers, the process of honoring the process. And finally, to remember that in the end, the mountains we've climbed will create one amazing landscape.

We are so much stronger than we know. We are equipped with everything we need to make it back to solid ground. It won't happen overnight, but it will happen. An everlasting pilot light of happiness burns within each of us that is our true nature. Fueling that flame, keeping it burning bright, and learning to turn it back up when it gets dim is at the center of the multifaceted skill of happiness.

You've got this. Even when it doesn't feel like it. Even when the heaviness feels unbearable. You are infinitely loved and supported. Know deeply that somehow, some way, you've got this, no matter what. Our greatest breakthroughs can emerge after our biggest breakdowns. Love yourself through it. The universe is behind you.

> *"Our greatest breakthroughs can emerge after our biggest breakdowns."*

Now we're moving on to Part II of this journey together! I'm excited to outline for you exactly where to begin adding even more bricks to your foundation for super-bright, sustainable happiness— by making over your mornings. It all begins with deliberately choosing and creating the kind of days you want to live from the very moment you wake up, thereby deliberately designing your life on a daily basis. This is the idea that created the single most dramatic positive transformation in my life, and I know it can for you, too. Here we go!

PART II

THE ESSENTIAL SHIFT:

MAKE OVER YOUR

MORNINGS

CHAPTER 4

Happiness Starts with Your First Thoughts of the Day

$\mathcal{I}$'m one of the happiest people I know. I love my life, live with passion, and wake up nearly every day excited about what's ahead. When I think of how it didn't used to be that way for me, how much I struggled for so many years, I'm filled with immense gratitude for all I've learned and the changes I've made.

This leads me to share with you the single most monumental and profound change I made to live and sustain the happiness I was looking for: *I changed the way I was living my mornings.*

For years, I was caught in a pattern of waking up thinking about the negative, the stressful, and the to-do list for the day. I was skipping breakfast (or worse, eating for breakfast what should actually be dessert), rushing to get out the door, taking zero time to be mindful or set my intentions for what I wanted my day—or my life—to look like. I just threw caution to the wind and left the outcome of my day to chance rather than work to consciously craft the day I desired from the moment I woke up. Millions of people live this way. It's an epidemic. I truly believe that much of the unhappiness in this world is due to the way people are starting their mornings.

There's even research to support this. For example, a University of Toronto study published in the American Psychological Association journal *Emotion* found in a survey of more than seven hundred participants ages seventeen to seventy-nine that those who consider themselves morning people generally feel happier and healthier than night owls.

When I went through my own huge transformation a few years back, I was so determined to create change, I began waking up each day and immediately focusing on quality, uplifting thoughts and actions that supported my happiness. When I first started, it felt a little unnatural because I was breaking out of old patterns that were so ingrained. But after a while, the positive changes and habits became second nature, and the most important bricks in the foundation of my happiness became solid. Later, when I was really studying and evaluating exactly what I did that created such positive, sustainable results, I realized that specifically changing my mornings had the biggest impact on changing my entire life.

When practicing the skill of happiness and creating the beautiful life you desire and deserve, this is exactly where to begin: your mornings. I can't emphasize this enough, which is why I've devoted an entire section of the book to it. The way we start each day essentially determines what kind of day we'll have and, therefore, what kind of life we'll have.

> *"The way we start each day essentially determines what kind of day we'll have and, therefore, what kind of life we'll have."*

Now it's not like this morning thing is a huge, undiscovered secret. Billionaire entrepreneurs, CEOs, powerful business strategists, and the world's most gifted spiritual leaders all prize their morning routines as the foundation for their success, happiness, and inner peace. They know that true success begins with authentic happiness (not the other way around) and that mornings are the time to make it happen. But incredibly, this concept is so massively overlooked, it goes completely undiscovered by most people.

From the time we're kids, we are conditioned to see mornings as rushed, hectic, stressful, and full of demands on our energy. We carry this into adulthood as the norm, without realizing the immense deficiency it's causing in our lives on every level.

When I'm teaching workshops or speaking to groups, one of the most common things people share with me is that they "get" all the positivity stuff and they know basically what's needed to create a happier life, but they feel a little overwhelmed by it all and aren't sure where to begin . . . so they don't. They get caught in a cycle of going to motivational classes and reading spiritual books without ever creating any significant change. This is why I am so passionate about helping you make over your mornings! This is a doable, tangible place for anyone to start implementing everything in a way that will have incredible impact and create the momentum needed for authentic, sustainable, positive change. Just start with your mornings, and I can promise you, you will change your life.

GENTLY SHIFTING OLD HABITS

Creating the changes in your mornings that will set the foundation for happiness and success throughout each day—and every day—takes heightened awareness. At first, you'll have to catch yourself when you veer off the path, but if you stick to it long enough, the flow will become natural.

My friend Amateo Ra, a super-wise spiritual teacher and business coach, has been working toward creating this powerful shift in his own life. He recently shared a relatable story with me that is a fantastic example of lovingly nudging yourself to course correct when you feel yourself slipping back into old habits.

Yesterday morning, I woke up and started my day in a hurry. I began cleaning, getting my day started, and soon was on social media and checking e-mail.

I quickly realized I had a sense of rush or hurriedness and could see it reflected in my surroundings. Our internal resonance creates our external reality. I quickly came to my senses and decided to do something drastic.

So I got back in bed and began to restart my day with gratitude, love, joy, rest, and grace. Oh, and some deep filling of my Source tank. After a full reset, I felt like a new person and ended up having an extremely productive, clear, and creative day. I totally crushed it.

Conscious living is about compassionate self-awareness. It's not about doing everything perfectly; it's about how to course correct on each step of life to get into the groove of what you truly desire.

While not everyone has the time on a busy weekday morning to crawl back into bed for longer than a minute or two, we all have the time and power to pause, reset, and consciously change paths when we become aware that the vibe we're on is not empowering us. Amateo's story is a great example of this awareness and how he created a shift that changed the course of his entire day. It's all about discovering what works for you and pulling those tools and practices out when you need them.

I'm starting the section on making over your mornings with this chapter on the tremendous power of your morning thoughts and how the happiness in your life begins with your first thoughts of the day. This is truly where it all starts. Then we'll have some fun in later chapters discussing ways to reinvent your morning routine, busting anxiety (and sleeping better), eating for happiness, and creating surroundings that support your joy. Ready to take some powerful action steps with me? Here we go!

THE POWER OF YOUR MORNING THOUGHTS

The energy, thoughts, and mind-sets we take on in the first minutes and hours of the day are carried with us throughout the day. A day that starts with feeling rushed, depleted, stressed out, and negative will ultimately turn out that way. Even if you think you're doing pretty well in this area, you might be surprised by how you can step it up even more and make a huge difference.

In Chapter 2, we covered thought management, and now we're going to go a little deeper, because the place to begin is in our very first thoughts of the day. These are some of the most influential and powerful thoughts in our lives, and mastering them can create major transformation.

As you're waking up each morning, those first few thoughts that float through your cloudy mind are some of your most powerful, and they set the stage for your entire day. With practice, you can teach yourself to shift your focus when you wake up to make your first thoughts of the day positive, inspiring, and high quality.

After I had surgery on my shoulder in 2008 and decided to use the recovery time to become happier once and for all, one of the first things I did was set an intention to see how I could change my thoughts in some areas.

I'd learned over the years through my research how powerful thoughts are, and knowing that simply changing the way you look at something can bring a whole new perspective, I began to look for patterns in my thoughts that could be contributing to the not-so-desirable place I'd been in for so long. I really wanted to identify some of the blocks that were preventing me from moving forward in the positive way I desired.

After carefully tuning in to my thought patterns for a few days, I noticed that when I was first opening my eyes in the morning, and even before that, many of the thoughts running through my mind were of stuff that made me feel instantly drained or bummed out. I was waking up with images of people who had recently caused me pain, projects that were dragging me down, obligations that weren't feeding my soul, and on it goes. I was getting out of bed and starting my day like that! No wonder I'd been in such a funk for so long!

If I could be more conscious of my very first thoughts in the morning and make a deliberate effort to be sure they were pleasant, positive, and healing, could that potentially change . . . everything?

I went on a mission to be very aware of my first thoughts upon waking. Could I teach myself to automatically wake up in a loving, nurturing state? For the next few weeks, as soon as I was awake in the morning, I immediately brushed off any negative thoughts that tried to creep in and challenged myself to replace them with something happy or inspiring.

We're all a little spacey when we first wake up, right? Well, I'm no exception. So upon waking, when I'd notice my thoughts, I'd work to remember my mission to think of positive thoughts and images in those moments, and then just allow my mind to flow to whatever happy things organically popped up: lemon drops, an excited dog barking in the distance, birds chirping, gratitude for how fantastically cozy the bed was. I focused on anything that would steer me away from any negative junk that tried to creep in.

The first few days were a bit challenging, and I caught myself straying to nasty places in my mind a few times, but as soon as I noticed it, I would quickly shift back to positive. It almost became like a fun game. And holy cow, some of the crap I discovered sneaking into my head in the morning was frightening!

As I woke up further, I would shift to more complex empowering thoughts, like *I'm going to create a great day today* (and then think about the "how"). I would also practice thinking positive, empowering affirmations that applied to the day ahead. Even on what seemed to be the hardest days, simple thoughts like *I'm thankful to be safe and in a calm, quiet place* were amazingly helpful.

After practicing this for a few weeks, I noticed it became easier, and I was getting out of bed not just in a happier place, but also in an amazingly blissful state. Everything seemed brighter, and when my feet hit the ground, I was ready and excited for a great day ahead. It all started to come naturally.

Some of the things that had been plaguing me before began to fall away. Clarity began to emerge, and new perspective set in. I was more productive and optimistic, and my days kept getting better and better. I even started to apply the positive thought practice during the day or in the evenings when I found myself slipping into the negative. I learned to brush off negative thoughts the same way I would shoo a fly.

After a month or so, the change in my morning thoughts became automatic. The happy morning thoughts, and therefore happy mornings and better days, became a permanent shift.

MORE THOUGHT-CHANGING TOOLS

Changing your first thoughts, as well as your routine in the morning, to bring in the positive is not only part of a fresh way to approach achieving a happier life, it's also a fundamental part of bringing more energy, optimism, and success into your world.

Here are a few helpful tools and ideas to help you create your daily practice of waking up in a positive, empowering place. I use them to keep me on track. I love them because they're super-simple and because they really work.

○ **Keep a pad and pen next to the bed to write down positive thoughts and affirmations when they come to mind.** When you need a little nudge in the morning, grab it and read away. You can also use this to write down those great ideas that pop into your head in the middle of the night and nag you until you either lose them forever (a major bummer) or write them down. Those are some of the brightest ideas, and it's important to capture them (not to mention, getting them on paper and out of your head brings instant peace).

○ **Memorize a favorite saying or affirmation as a default phrase you can shift to when needed.** One of my favorites is "It's a brand-new day and another opportunity to create joy and success."

○ **Keep a favorite quote or affirmation in a frame on your night-stand.** This will always put you in a better place. I have a quote I love from Neale Donald Walsch that reads, "If you want the best the world has to offer, offer the world your best."

○ **Keep a glass of water next to your bed so it's waiting for you when you wake up.** The water will be there to welcome you to the new day, refresh your body, and start you off in a nurtured place. It's a physical reminder that you should do loving things for yourself. I can't stress enough how important it is to give your body the gift of hydration. Hydration = energy! We'll be talking about that more in Chapter 7.

○ **Subscribe to a positive blog or newsletter so you have a regular flow of uplifting content to read anytime you need it.** I've made a habit of reading at least one every morning when I have my tea or coffee. Do this before you open yourself up to whatever the current news headlines are that day. They can wait. You can use the daybook section starting on page 175 to begin creating the habit of daily positive reading. I've also included a few of my favorite Web sites for positive reading in Suggested Reading on page 245.

THE THREE S'S

Oh, how I'm excited to share this one with you! It's a simple tool I originally created for myself as a simple way to get into the right mind-set each morning. I found it worked so well that I started teaching it, and it has become one of the most popular practices I share. It's quick, super-powerful, super-easy, and when practiced enough, it becomes second nature to reach for it in the mornings or whenever you need to hit your inner reset button. I've received tons of e-mails about how this has created big change for people (which lights up my heart).

I'm big on simplicity, and nothing gets me inspired more than super-simple tools that produce kick-ass results. The Three S's is definitely one of those.

How to Do the Three S's

You can do this when you wake in the morning (I like to do it while I'm still in bed resting, paying attention to the sounds of the birds outside, etc.) or any time of day you're feeling stressed or need a mini-break or a change in energy.

Close your eyes and do these three things—in order—and feel the shift! It only takes a minute or two, but it can change the course of your whole day and attract amazing things!

Smile. Science has shown that the simple, physical act of cracking a smile triggers the release of the chemical dopamine in the brain, which creates a feel-good state. It even works if you're faking the smile, so if you need to, fake it till you make it! Hold it for around thirty seconds. When you feel a shift in your energy, move on to the second S. Try holding the smile through the next two S's for maximum impact and to keep the energy flowing.

Say thanks. The energy of gratitude is amazing! Take a minute now to think about what you're grateful for in this moment. Picture some of these things in your mind's eye if you can (favorite people, favorite foods, simple pleasures, your warm bed, etc.). Feel the positive transformation that comes from shifting your mind-set to a place of gratitude. This sets the fuel for the next S. When you feel ready, move on to the final S.

Set an intention. Now that you've created a positive shift in your heart and mind through smiling and saying thanks, it's time to set an intention. It can be general, such as "I intend to enjoy today and spend time with people who inspire me." It can be specific, like "I intend to be a valuable contributor in today's office meeting, and my ideas will be well received." One of my favorites is "I intend to take excellent care of my mind and body today and to inspire others to do the same." The first two S's not only put energetic fuel behind your intention, they also help connect you to your soul so your intention can come from deep within, which really helps it stick.

That's it! Open your eyes and go about the rest of your day with better energy, a brighter outlook, and a clear intention. Keep the Three S's in your happiness toolbox and bust them out anytime you need them. See if you can turn this into a new daily habit. Remember: Small shifts create miracles!

CHAPTER 5

Reinventing Your Morning Routine

I can vividly remember one stressful morning several years ago that, sadly, was somewhat typical for me at that time. I was awake staring at the clock at 3:17 a.m. My mind was spinning. An 8:00 a.m. meeting with a possible new PR client was looming, and I'd barely slept. Rampant thoughts were running through my head. *I want to wear that black wrap dress, but did I pick it up from the cleaners? I can't remember. Damn, it might rain, and if it does, traffic will be a nightmare. This comforter is so freakin' hot! I'm thirsty, but if I get up now, I'll never get back to sleep. This sucks.* Somehow, I did manage to drift back to sleep for a while.

The alarm woke me at 6:00 a.m.; its well-meaning, cheerful chimes were an unwelcome irritation. I sat up in the bed, trying to muster the motivation to hop to it. *Ugh!* I thought, as I realized it was indeed raining outside. I had less than an hour to get out the door.

Knowing I needed to leave at least a half-hour earlier because of the rain, I rinsed birdbath-style in the shower but didn't wash my hair. Instead I threw it into a ponytail, wrapped myself in a towel, and started to rifle through my closet for the black dress I wanted to wear. It was still at the cleaners. I put on a "plan B" dress, which I didn't feel my best in, but I knew it would work.

As I finished getting ready, I realized I was battling the clock. No time to drink coffee or eat. How I wished I had a Starbucks barista in the house in that moment. I jetted out the door without a moment to spare.

A few minutes later, sitting in the usual gridlocked L.A. traffic, I started to breathe a little better, realizing I was on my way and telling myself I could hit a drive-thru after the meeting for coffee and food. I was reaching for the radio to catch the news when I realized with horror that I'd left the sticky note with the address for the meeting on it sitting on my desk. "You can't be serious!" I screamed at the top of my lungs, blood rushing into my cheeks. I must have frightened the guy sitting next to me in traffic.

I took a breath and sat in silence for a minute, inching along in the rain with no way in sight to exit the freeway, and started to quietly whimper. I'd had it.

I knew that I'd be very late at this point, and that even if I could make it on time, I was in no mental state to deliver a presentation to a new client. I left a message saying something had come up and I needed to reschedule. Relieved, I headed back home.

Looking back on that hectic morning, and the rampant mediocrity of my mornings overall back then, I clearly see how I was not only responsible for the way it all went, but I actually created it! The way I was choosing to live my mornings was the primary cause of so much of the stress, anxiety, and depleted joy levels. My own lack of a supportive morning routine combined with occasional poor planning was causing me to start many days running on empty.

You don't have to have mornings as hectic as that one for them to negatively affect your life. The all-too-common hurried, slightly stressed, mentally-repeating-the-day's-to-do-list kind of mornings are sneaky. They seem okay, but they're really draining your energy and joy rather than serving as the incredible fuel they could be. Mediocrity in this area, or any area, doesn't work when it comes to creating the life you desire. The goal is to create shifts to your mornings so they can be the most powerful, supportive fuel for your happiest, most successful life—like filling the gas tank, rotating the tires, and changing the oil in your car before a road trip.

When I changed my mornings, the positive impact on my entire life was immediate. I've never looked back. As a result, I consistently have so much more energy, peace, clarity. My morning routine is the sacred firewood that ignites my life.

> *"When I changed my mornings, the positive impact on my entire life was immediate. I've never looked back."*

The first couple of hours of each day are when I apply a large percentage of my planning, deliberate positive thinking, and healthy practices. These are key areas to focus on that have the most impact. We've covered morning thoughts (the number-one area to work on), and now we'll dig further into adjusting routine, improving sleep, busting anxiety, eating super-powered happiness foods, and creating spaces that support happiness. This stuff is not only life changing—it's also fun! We're going to be creative and get you trying out some new things, and who doesn't love that?

Taking an honest look at how your mornings currently unfold is a great place to start. Then, you'll be in a great place to begin a morning makeover. This simple questionnaire I've created for you will help you answer some important questions about how you're starting your day and get a better picture of where you could make your first changes. You can fill it in here, or if you'd like, I've created a printable download (along with some other helpful tools) on my Web site at kristiling.com/operationhappinessresources. Ready for your morning makeover? Let's get started. Remember, the idea is to go from *tolerating* to *enjoying* on all levels.

TIME IS ON YOUR SIDE (IF YOU ALLOW IT TO BE)

Let's talk about how much time you have to get ready in the morning. This is an area where most of us can use improvement. I was *so* guilty

Your Morning Assessment Worksheet

Do I allow myself enough time in the morning to get ready at a peaceful and reasonable pace?

☐   ☐   ☐
Yes! I allow myself   **No**   **Could do better**
plenty of time.

Am I getting enough sleep on a regular basis to wake up and face the day in a healthy, refreshed, energetic way?

☐   ☐   ☐
For sure! I get plenty   **No**   **Could do better**
of quality sleep.

Do I eat something healthy and drink plenty of water in the morning to give my body the nutrients and hydration it needs to get going?

☐   ☐   ☐
Yes! I eat a healthy   **No**   **Could do better**
breakfast.

Are my bedroom and bathroom organized in a way that makes it easy to find what I need when getting ready?

☐   ☐   ☐
Yes! I get ready   **No**   **Could do better**
with ease.

Does the space I wake up to and get ready in nurture me and make me feel good?

☐   ☐   ☐
Yes! I love where I   **No**   **Could do better**
wake up daily.

of the morning rush for so long! Even if you're waking up and giving yourself plenty of time to get ready and out the door on time, are you allowing yourself the luxury of a little extra time to read a motivating article, meditate or enjoy some stillness (even for a couple of minutes), lovingly connect in a meaningful way with a pet or family member, or step outside for some healing deep breaths of fresh air?

Is my commute enjoyable and filled with music I like, positive audio-books, or uplifting talk radio?

☐ **Yes! I have a peaceful commute.**   ☐ **No**   ☐ **Could do better**

Do I allow myself enough time to wake up fully and breathe a bit before jumping on social media or e-mail?

☐ **Yes, at least a few minutes.**   ☐ **No**   ☐ **Could do better**

Overall, do I feel I could benefit from a more positive, peaceful morning routine?

☐ **Yes! It would make a big difference.**   ☐ **No**   ☐ **Could do better**

If you answered *no* or *could do better* on four or more of the questions, you're definitely in need of a few positive changes. Even if your answers were mostly *yes*, you'll likely find some ideas and suggestions in this section that will help you take your mornings to a new level.

If you're beginning to realize you could use some reorganizing and rethinking to get your days started in a happier, more supportive way, the rest of this section will offer solutions and ideas to help create more joyful, organized mornings that will lead you into more empowered days.

I get up much earlier than I need to each morning because I value that time so much. And if I have to be at the airport or an early appointment, I figure out what time I think I need to be up and set the alarm on my phone for thirty minutes earlier than that. Once I'm up and moving, I thank myself every time.

To start adding more "you time" to your mornings, try setting your alarm to wake you up just fifteen minutes earlier than you usually do. It may take a few days to adjust, but it's so worth it. And whatever you do, avoid that surly snooze button—it's not your friend.

If fifteen minutes seems like a challenge, start with five and work up to fifteen. Even just five extra minutes in the morning can make a big difference, especially if you have kids that will need your attention. These little slices of your time are a basic element in creating more happiness and balance. They can really amp up your sense of harmony and empowerment. Setting aside just five minutes of stillness and quiet in the morning to connect with yourself, your spirit, and your life is immensely powerful and clarifying.

And on that note, I'll mention that giving yourself five extra minutes in many areas of your life is an amazingly powerful practice. I actually work to be five minutes early whenever possible, wherever I'm going. It gives me time to sit and chill out for a few minutes before an appointment, and if some unexpected obstacle pops up on my way (like traffic), it gives a cushion that takes away so much stress. It's kind of amazing how much drama this small change has zapped from my life. It's a small shift that makes a big difference.

How to Best Manage Your Time

Let's chat for a bit about time management. I'd like to share three of the best time-management tips I've picked up along my path. They not only apply to your mornings but will support you in many other areas of your life. These tips are awesome and may even surprise you. Truly, sometimes you can actually get more done (and better!) by doing less, because you'll be focused on your most important priorities with fewer distractions and less stress. Think of great time-management practices as an important part of the skill of happiness. They'll not only create more breathing room, they'll help you direct your precious energy to the things that are truly important to you (and make it easier to ditch the rest).

Be mindful about multitasking. Mornings are prime time for multitasking, but believe it or not, it's not always productive or helpful. I used to be the queen of multitasking, but I've since realized that it was not serving me the way I thought it was. In fact, it was holding me back and taking away from my enjoyment of little things.

When we're multitasking, we're not fully present for any of the tasks we're trying to accomplish. It's best not to multitask on anything you wish to give your full attention to. I enjoy making coffee in the morning—I find the process meditative and relaxing. So, I don't do anything else at the same time. If you have kids, try being fully present while getting them ready, rather than checking social media or throwing in loads of laundry. The joy you'll get from that couple of minutes of quality time is so much more valuable than the minute or two you save by multitasking.

Examine where you multitask and ask yourself if it's supportive or draining, and then make changes accordingly. Try creating a list of areas in your life where you know you multitask, then mark each one as either supportive or draining. Some examples: Brushing your teeth in the shower (supportive and time-saving). Doing squats while brushing your teeth (supportive and . . . awesome!). Making breakfast while checking e-mail (draining). Talking on the phone while picking out your clothes (draining—and may result in some scary fashion choices you'll regret later in the day).

Slow down. It may seem counterproductive when it comes to time management, but believe it or not, slowing down just a little in everything you do can actually be a time-saver and help you be more on target, as well as allow you to be more present in everything. And presence is a major happiness booster.

> " . . . believe it or not, slowing down just a little in everything you do can actually be a time-saver and help you be more on target."

Simply slowing down helps prevent lost keys, forgotten coats, and even injury. Honestly, every time I can remember being injured over the past few years, it was because I was going too fast. A couple years ago, I was loading some things into the back of a friend's Jeep. I was moving so quickly (for no good reason) that I didn't notice the back hatch hadn't gone up all the way due to a faulty spring. I stood up full speed right into it, gaining me a trip to my local urgent-care center, where the doctor put eight staples into my melon. Fun. I realized that night I'd been moving way too fast across the board for some time and received the smack on my head as a message to slow way down.

Slowing down in general brings a sense of more peace, clarity, and mindfulness to everything we do. It's not just about presence, but pleasure as well. It helps you savor moments, create more joyful memories, and notice beautiful details in the *now* that might otherwise have been overlooked in your hurriedness. It makes a huge difference in your overall quality of life. Go slower. Learn to pause more. Step off the hamster wheel. Take time to breathe.

Try creating a list of ways you could slow down and how it might make a positive difference in your day. Perhaps you might carve out an extra couple of minutes to enjoy your breakfast, or give yourself extra time to style your hair. Even the smallest things can make a big difference.

Chunk your time. Divide your time into bite-size increments to dedicate fully to each task. Give yourself loving permission to unplug from distractions and focus on only one task during each section of time without being pulled in a million different directions. This is a huge stress-buster and is actually a major time-saver. For example, I set aside a few hours this morning to work on this book. From 7:00 a.m. to 10:00 a.m, I'm doing nothing but writing this section about how to make time work in our favor. By setting my goal (1,200 words for today) and allowing a chunk of time to give it complete focus, I'll have no problem getting it done. It's not just drive and enthusiasm that make great things happen, it's also focus and presence.

Setting aside specific sections of time is also a great way to plan out amazingly supportive mornings. How long do you want to sit and enjoy your coffee or tea or stretch or move your body? Chunking some time for this (even just a couple of minutes) guarantees you get that precious, soulful time and also makes it guilt-free (the best part). You can apply this same idea to getting dressed, reading something uplifting, caring for loved ones, checking e-mails and social media, and making sure you have time to nourish your body and spirit. It works great for getting things done at the office, too.

How many times can we remember thinking at the end of a day, *Wow, I was super-busy today, but it doesn't seem like I got much done! This* method is the way to get things done and reduce busyness. A win-win!

Here's a chart that will give you a snapshot of what a typical morning could look like if you had ninety minutes from the time you woke up until you needed to be out the door. You can chunk your time so you can fully focus and enjoy each activity. This is just an example, but I do recommend sketching out a custom chart like this for yourself based on your own needs.

7:00 a.m. to 8:05 a.m.	Wake, drink water, breathe fresh air, stretch, say hello to loved ones.
8:05 a.m. to 8:20 a.m.	Make and enjoy tea or coffee and have a healthy bite, read or listen to something uplifting.
8:20 a.m. to 8:30 a.m.	Pick out and style your outfit for the day.
8:30 a.m. to 9:10 a.m.	Shower, get dressed, do hair and makeup (if you wear any).
9:10 a.m. to 9:30 a.m.	Assist any family members who need help getting out the door, check social media and e-mail.

SMALL SHIFTS, BIG RESULTS

Making over your mornings, and any other area of life, is all about small shifts, big results. So that's what we're creating here: Small changes that, with practice and dedication, will result in powerful positive change. Try the ideas and suggestions that feel good and doable to you, along with a few of your own, and you'll notice an immediate difference in the quality of your days. As soon as you begin, you'll notice your outlook, energy levels, and overall state of mind will be bumped up a notch.

It's a great idea to get started right away (if you haven't already) on creating the changes you know will improve your mornings in big ways. Starting now with small steps will get the ball rolling and create momentum to go a bit deeper, which we'll be doing in the next two chapters. There's so much good stuff still to come. Keep in mind that happiness is a renewable resource, and mornings are the best place to keep it renewed!

CHAPTER 6

Rest, Relaxation, and Reducing Anxiety

Before we get started, I'd like to share that this chapter, and the next chapter on love-centered eating and wellness, are really applicable to all areas of life, as are many of the ideas I share in this section of the book. However, I believe the first place to begin tackling these things and creating the momentum needed for all positive change is in the morning. Starting each day with a bright scope of supportive practices, mind-sets, and habits that can be carried throughout the whole day and night with ease is the way to the greatest success in so many areas. In this sense, mornings really are the foundation for most everything we wish to heal, feel, or accomplish in our lives.

Anxiety really tends to show up in ways that can put a big damper on our mornings. Much of the time, it creeps in when we're trying to get to sleep at night, robbing us of needed rest and leading us to wake up exhausted. It also tends to pop up first thing in the morning when we allow worrisome thoughts about the day ahead to get the best of us. This is why the morning is a great place to begin incorporating anxiety-busting practices that help guide us onto a positive track for the day—and evening—ahead.

REDUCING AND EMBRACING ANXIETY

When I was thirty-one, I found myself suffering from a number of random, annoying health issues, such as insomnia, exhaustion, knots in my stomach much of the time, and just an overall sense of unwellness and stress. I had a doctor at the time whom I adored, and I decided to go see him to share how tired I was of feeling that way. Admittedly, I went to whine, really, but it turned out to be a life-changing visit.

"How long have you been feeling this way?" he asked.

I hadn't really thought about how long it had been going on. But in that moment, I realized I'd been living in that state on and off for so long, it kind of seemed like the norm to me. "Well, for a while, I guess. Years?" I said, feeling slightly defeated.

"Years?! Has anyone ever told you that this is anxiety? I think it's a pretty severe case of generalized anxiety disorder. We can work on this; you just need to make some changes." It was the first time I realized that the worrisome mind-sets and knots in my stomach that were keeping me up at night actually had a specific name.

I hadn't really thought of anxiety as its own ailment before. I mean, I knew of the word *anxiety* and thought it was basically just another term for stress. How wrong I was, and my doc was absolutely right. Although they often go hand in hand, stress and anxiety are different. Stress can cause anxiety, but sometimes anxiety just creeps in on its own due to emotional, environmental, or other factors that can be hard to detect. This can seriously deflate our sense of happiness and peace. Anxiety affects most everyone from time to time, and chronic anxiety like I used to have affects millions of people. According to the Anxiety and Depression Association of America, 18 percent of US adults suffer from some kind of anxiety disorder, costing billions each year to treat.

With stress, we're normally pretty clear on what it is that's freaking us out—a test, a deadline, a strained relationship. We can usually finish the sentence "I'm totally stressed because of _____." With anxiety, we often feel restless and high-strung without immediately knowing why we're feeling that way, making it harder to fix the problem and feel centered again.

Like stress, anxiety has an acute adverse effect on our quality of life. Sometimes it's situational and sometimes it's just in general, which was the case with me. I realized I could change it by identifying and dealing with the causes rather than just staying stuck in a cycle of trying to temporarily relieve the symptoms. Deep breathing, exercise, and meditation are all wonderful (and highly recommended for multiple reasons), but I've found they usually treat the symptoms of anxiety rather than the cause, so for the best results, more action is needed to narrow down the cause.

When I became determined to eliminate anxiety from my life as much as possible, I knew that the first step would be to find some clear way to turn inward and easily identify the core cause of why I was feeling anxious. Although it took me several years of research, perseverance, and personal trial and error, I was finally able to reduce my anxiety by about 97 percent (a smidgen of anxiety can actually be a healthy thing and is totally normal). When I think about it, I'm still completely blown away by the tremendous difference this has made in my life and the happiness it's created the space for. I now embrace any anxiety that does show up as a message from my soul that I need to examine something. Thinking of it this way is immensely empowering.

I'm going to show you just how to help yourself nail down the cause of anxiety right when you notice it by examining a few specific areas, so you can address what's going on by taking action. Action is the true, best remedy for relieving anxiety, but first you must be clear on where to direct the effort.

This is mighty stuff, and what I really love about it is that it's also amazingly uncomplicated. Even if you don't suffer from anxiety in the severe way I did for so long, this will be super-helpful to you on the occasions it does creep in. Connecting the dots between the anxiety and the cause empowers you to go straight to the root of the issue and take action to dissolve it.

So let's get into how to connect those dots so you can add this awesomeness to your happiness toolbox. The process I'm about to share with you will not only help you greatly reduce anxiety (and stress) but it will also lead to heightened self-awareness about your true needs and desires and help you expand your happiness by eliminating energy drains.

THE THREE PRIMARY CAUSES OF ANXIETY

I've found that most anxiety is caused by one (or more) of just three primary factors. For some, there are other factors in the mix such as genetics, past trauma, or certain medical conditions, but for most, these three are the key. And at the risk of ruffling a few feathers, I'd like to share that I was told more than once that my severe anxiety was likely genetic; in spite of that, using these three factors *still* worked for me! While genetics certainly play a factor in many elements of our makeup, I don't believe they have to rule over our quality of life; we get to do that.

When I started linking any anxiety (and even some stress) I was experiencing to things in my life that fell under these three categories, an entirely new world opened up for me. When you're experiencing symptoms of anxiety (sleepless nights, nervous energy, knots in your stomach), check in with yourself to see if you have something going on that falls under one of the causes I share here.

1. **Neglecting your self-care.** This is like a vitamin deficiency of the spirit. Neglected self-care can deflate us in all areas. It can be as small as badly needing a haircut or having chipped nail polish (seriously!) or as big as putting off a trip to the dermatologist to have a suspicious spot checked. It can mean you know you've been eating like crap for days or just that you haven't been get-

ting enough sleep. When we get busy, it's easy to let our self-care wheels fall off, but this only leads to chaos. When you feel yourself off track here, immediately make some shifts and change course. It will make a huge difference and help alleviate the anxiety that comes from self-neglect.

In addition to paying closer attention to neglected self-care, I encourage you to examine your life and look at ways you can step up your self-care across the board. I did this in a big way years ago in my happiness journey, and it's made a huge difference. I retrained my mind to make taking care of myself a higher priority, adding things like spending time daily outside in nature (even a couple of minutes makes a difference); monthly massages; and small, spontaneous ten-minute workouts several times a week.

I also began more mindfully guarding where I was exerting my physical and emotional energy (this was a big one). When these and other small shifts became habits, they amplified my level of happiness and helped to decrease anxiety and stress in all areas of my life. And since they were small changes, it was totally doable.

I can't emphasize enough how important daily self-care is in increasing and supporting lasting happiness in your life. Caring for your own body, mind, and spirit is your greatest (and grandest) responsibility. It's about listening to the needs of your soul and then honoring them. It's about recharging so you can shine your light and be your best for everyone and everything around you.

> "Caring for your own body, mind, and spirit is your greatest (and grandest) responsibility. It's about listening to the needs of your soul and then honoring them."

Be very careful not to allow life to become so busy that you fall into the mind-set that it's okay to put off taking care of yourself. This is spirit-crushing territory and one of the major cracks in the foundation that can take away from the sustainability of your happiness and peace. If your schedule is too packed to live fully, it's time for a change. Give yourself permission to do small, loving things for yourself daily, to pamper yourself regularly, and to say no to things that don't make your heart sing.

To help stay on track with your self-care during busy times, pause each morning to ask yourself these questions:

Am I hydrated?

Am I centered?

Do I have needs that are being put off?

Those three questions can help you check in with yourself regularly and quickly determine what might need attention so you can take steps to support your happiness, bust anxiety, and turn up the volume on your peace and joy. Nobody can take care of your beautiful, incredible self like you can!

2. **Obsessing over things that haven't even happened yet (and probably won't at all).** This is a major one, and it's really about losing track of being in the *now*. When we stress over what-ifs and fear of what might happen instead of focusing on the present and what actually *is*, we allow fear of things that don't even exist yet to rob us of our peace, joy, and even our power to consciously direct a situation to unfold the way we'd like it to.

A couple of years ago, when I first moved into my new house, I woke up one morning after a rainy night to find a big wet spot on the ceiling in my dining room. I'd just had the electrical system redone, and I knew they did some work on the roof right above that area. I freaked out right away and started future tripping on all the what-ifs . . . *What if there are exposed wires up there? What if there's mold already? What if the ceiling caves in?!*

I paced around nervously, and anxiety started to set in. It was only 6:30 a.m., so it was too early to call the contractor. I sat down to collect my thoughts and mull over what to do, and something came over me. I burst into laughter right there on my living room couch for the silliness I was creating! None of those things actually existed that I knew of, yet I was allowing my mind—and physical body—to act and feel as if they did, causing me to needlessly stress out and jump on the anxiety train. It was just a spot on the ceiling, and that's all. Nothing more.

That morning, I allowed myself a moment to happily take credit for catching what I was doing, because years ago, the old me would have just kept on stressing about all the what-ifs and let it ruin my day or week. Instead, this time, I caught myself and mindfully took control of the situation, squashing anxiety before it took over. I took a few deep breaths, made some coffee, and a little while later called the contractor. He fixed the leak and painted the ceiling at no charge, and all was well again.

The leak in my roof is a small example, but the idea here applies across all areas. Sometimes, major things such as illness, a financial setback, or other crisis can give you legitimate reason to be concerned. But staying calm and allowing yourself to be mindfully concerned while also staying in the moment and focusing on what *actually is* right now can help you keep a handle on your clarity and peace, even in the most challenging situations.

This practice helped me greatly last year when my younger brother went in for a very dangerous surgery to fix a tear in his carotid artery from a skiing accident. I sat in the hospital waiting room focusing on the fact that he was young, strong, and still okay in each moment that went by. I set the intention that all would be okay and that he would soon be recovering, surrounded by family.

When he came out of surgery and we realized everything went well, I was relieved and felt grateful that I'd remained in a state of peaceful energy and stillness as much as possible. Not just so things were better for me, but also so that I could offer the best support for my brother and my family. Hysterics and worry never help a situation, but peaceful energy, staying in the moment, and positive thoughts always do. If we consciously allow it, we get to choose what we bring to the table. This can make a huge difference in how we experience all the ups and downs that occur in our lives.

> *"Hysterics and worry never help a situation, but peaceful energy, staying in the moment, and positive thoughts always do."*

3. **Having unfinished business.** Believe it or not, this is possibly one of the biggest anxiety fire-starters there is. All the things we put off add up to drain our energy, cause worry, keep us up at night, and put a damper on our existence. Clutter, difficult conversations yet to be had, paperwork that needs to be done, and things that need to be repaired are all examples.

   As tempting as it is to put these things off, they are peace-suckers that can add up to put a major damper on our joy. Training ourselves to regularly take inventory of the little (and big) stuff that's looming, and then diligently creating the space to get those things taken care of, is life changing. This is also a great self-care practice.

   I'm fierce about not letting unfinished stuff weigh me down and drain my positive energy. I didn't used to be, but once I began regularly checking in with my life and zapping lingering stuff before it zapped me, that all changed, and a huge chunk of anxiety disappeared from my world.

   Take a few moments each day to turn inward and examine what you're tolerating, then create plans of action to reduce, delegate, or eliminate. Make a habit of this, and you will create more light, more peace, and more free time in your life.

The goal is to create shifts and habits that keep unfinished business in your life to a minimum. I've worked hard on this one, making some great changes in this area that have made a huge positive difference. I'm still not perfect and that's okay (I almost always file for an extension on my tax returns), but I'm conscious of it and that has made all the difference. I no longer put off difficult conversations (but I do approach them with love), I take note of little things that need taken care of and then get them done, and I've studied and gained awesome time-management skills that have helped me create a healthy balance. Empowering!

> *"The goal is to create shifts and habits that keep unfinished business in your life to a minimum."*

Next time you feel anxiety ruling your day, ask yourself if you have one or more of the following in play: *neglecting your self-care, obsessing over things that haven't happened yet, or having unfinished business.* If you use the clarity you gain to empower you to take action and tell anxiety that you're in control, you'll notice an astonishing and rapid change. This simple process has changed my life.

SLEEP: IT'S LIKE CANDY, ONLY BETTER

My brother has a pet tortoise called Mrs. T that slips under his house and peacefully hibernates for three months out of the year. I seriously think she's on to something. Let's face it: A bad night's sleep sucks and negatively affects your whole day. If you're in the habit of regularly starting your days with a sleep deficit, this is a major bliss-blocker in your life.

We all get a crappy night's sleep from time to time, and some of us (including me on occasion) have suffered from bouts of insomnia, which can be maddening. Improving your quality of sleep can bring drastic improvements in every area. Sleep is when our body renews itself. It's when we heal, and it's when our minds clear. We simply can't live our very best lives without enough of it.

I used to have such bad insomnia (fueled by anxiety) that I would often go through a day on just an hour or two of sleep. Most other days, I was only getting five to seven hours, which, over time, is just not enough. When I dedicated myself to researching and practicing radical happiness a few years back, part of that was looking at what can improve my sleep. I was so over tossing and turning, and I knew that making some deliberate changes in that area would be hugely supportive all around.

All of us, at one time or another, have trouble sleeping. When it happens, tons of factors could be in play. They could be issues with diet, lack of exercise, anxiety, or all three (triple whammy). The great news is that when you learn and implement supportive habits that positively impact quality of sleep, as well as learn about and avoid what can screw it up, you can create immediate change in this area. In some ways, it's helpful to think of sleep as a skill—just like happiness.

By applying the anxiety-busting concepts we talked about in the last section, you can start getting better rest right away. And you can do a number of other supportive things that can make a huge difference in the sleep department.

Here are a few of my favorites.

○ **If your mind is racing when you're trying to get to sleep, make lists of ten random positive things in your mind.** Healthy things you ate that day, things you're feeling grateful for that day, little things you're looking forward to the next day, etc. This will occupy your mind and calm you. When I do this, I often fall asleep before I get to ten. If you get to ten and you're still awake, start on another list.

○ **Avoid eating for a minimum of two hours before going to bed.** If you can make it three or longer, even better. Changing the kinds of foods you eat for dinner can help as well. Stick with a light, veggie-heavy dinner. In the next chapter, we'll be covering all kinds of juicy shifts and ideas about food that will help you here as well.

○ **Quit the TV and other electronic devices at least thirty minutes before you crash out.** I know this is a tough one, but it will give your eyes a chance to wind down from all that light, movement, and random information. Spend that last time of the day reading, meditating, making lists, or doing small tasks around the house (I personally like to wipe down my kitchen and get the coffeemaker ready for the next morning). If checking social media before bed is too tempting, be sure to have your device on the lowest brightness setting and try to keep the time you spend on it to a minimum.

○ **Take a few minutes to read something positive before turning off the light.** Pick a chapter from an uplifting book or a positive magazine. This will put your mind in a peaceful place to drift off.

○ **Evaluate the bed you sleep in.** Is it old and saggy? Are you madly in love with your sheets and blankets? You should be! Are you waking up with a stiff neck because your pillow is too flat? Your bed should be a sacred, heavenly place. My life changed when I discovered the combination of a high-quality mattress and organic cotton jersey sheets—it's like sleeping on a squishy T-shirt! Run, don't walk, to the nearest bed and bath store and see what speaks to you. You spend about a third of your entire life in bed—it's worth investing in.

○ **Make sure your room is completely dark.** The darker the better. Even the tiniest bit of light through windows or from electronics can affect your sleep. I was amazed how much better I started sleeping when I installed blackout curtains a few years ago. When I travel, I even go as far as to stick rolled-up towels at the base of hotel room doors to keep the bright light out. It works!

○ **Keep electronics in your room to a minimum and as far away from you as you can while you're sleeping.** Everything is energy, including your sleep patterns. Keep anything that could possibly put a ripple in that energy at a safe distance.

MOVING FORWARD

While I touched on this earlier, I really want to emphasize that so much of our stress, anxiety, and overall uneasiness in life comes from ignoring what our souls are trying to communicate to us beneath the surface. By embracing feelings of anxiety and uneasiness as red flags from your inner voice, you can use them as prompts to take a deeper look at what really needs to be addressed, and what your authentic truth is in that moment. Mornings are an especially good time to turn inward and examine our inner whispers, as our minds tend to be clear and open to receiving. This mindful approach and heightened self-awareness is a tremendous gift we can give ourselves, and it can make a monumental positive difference across the board.

CHAPTER 7

The Love-Centered Diet: Eating to Support Your Happiest, Healthiest Life

When I think about the junk I used to put into my poor body, I cringe. For years, I ate fast food, drank too much, and overloaded on sugar without any idea what it was doing to my body, my mind, or my spirit. It didn't occur to me until later in life that all that toxic eating was directly linked to my anxiety, illness, and bouts of depression—not to mention the primary cause of the frustrating fatigue I experienced all through my twenties.

Our bodies are our ultimate source of renewable energy. They are beautiful miracles made up of trillions of tiny little universes called cells that rely solely on our love, support, and nurturing to thrive, and in return, support us in this life. I can't imagine a person on this earth whose body is not their single most prized possession, yet rare is the person who remembers this daily and lives in alignment with that priority.

This chapter is not your typical chapter on nutrition, health, and diet. It's a delicious little journey into shifting the way we make everyday choices, including food choices. It's not about a standard diet plan either, but rather a simple, mindful, love-centered, holistic lifestyle practice that can change the way we view the foods we're choosing and influence other choices we make—as we're making these choices. This makes it infinitely easier to pass up things that don't support our happiness and true desires for our best life and create the space to invite in more of those foods (and other things) that do.

I'm beyond excited to share this with you, because in its great simplicity lies tremendous transformational power. A small mind-set shift is all it takes to open up a new, empowering way to make even the smallest choices that impact your health, energy, and life.

Millions of people have been searching for decades for a miracle pill that will help them have more energy, release excess weight, and feel healthier when, in reality, this simple, mindful lifestyle path is the miracle they truly need. It's a powerful practice based on self-love that greatly strengthens our willpower and desire to make incredibly healthy, energizing choices like never before. A truly Love-Centered Diet.

I believe the weight-loss and health-care industries have something largely backward. Most of them tell people that if they lose weight, they'll feel great, look great, be healthier and happier, and have boundless energy. They work to convince us that we need whatever it is they're selling so we can lose the weight and achieve those desired results. Here's my question: What if we reverse it? I believe that if we consciously focus our efforts and choices first on just the desired results of being healthier and happier, feeling great, loving ourselves more, and having incredible energy—and we make those goals a top priority through radical self-care and choices aligned with these desires—our beautiful, intelligent, responsive bodies will feel safe to naturally seek out and maintain a healthy weight.

The fitness and weight-loss industries are correct that what we eat and drink and how much we move our bodies has an impact on what kind of physical and emotional shape we're in. But all that is part of simply loving ourselves and making definitive choices that support the amazing lives we desire and deserve.

MEET ME AT SUNRISE

The way you nourish your body in the morning drastically affects your entire day and, therefore, your life, which is why I chose to include this chapter in the section about making over your mornings. Mornings are where it all begins.

When we make powerful, nutrition-rich choices in the morning, it gives us the energy and mental clarity we need to create our best possible day. It also tends to set us on a great path to make healthier choices throughout the rest of the day, similar to the way we don't want to mess up the house right after we've spent hours cleaning it.

I'd like to share what led me to conceive and fall so madly in love with this Love-Centered Diet concept, while explaining the powerful mind-set shift and practice that is the heart of how it works. It's all based on one magical, potent question.

Powerful Question, Big Results

A while back, I was sitting in my studio one sunny afternoon working on a blog post about the power of our choices—how being intensely conscious about making choices that align with our hearts' true desires can change the course of our lives and light the path to everything we dream of. As I was writing, I thought, what if we asked ourselves *this* question before we make each choice, small or large: Is this choice in alignment with my heart's true desires for my best life?

> " . . . what if we asked ourselves _this_ question
> before we make each choice, small or large:
> Is this choice in alignment with my
> heart's true desires for my best life?"

A breeze was softly blowing through the curtains behind my desk, and my dogs, Venus and Ellis, were sleeping in the corner, enjoying every minute of this perfectly peaceful day. It dawned on me then how truly life changing this simple question can be when we dedicate ourselves to passionately putting it into practice on a consistent basis.

Of course, we all try, for the most part, to make choices that line up with what we want, but we don't always stop to check in with our inner voices and truly consider things on a holistic level. So many small choices, especially those involving food and our health, are made to gain instant gratification rather than to achieve the desired big-picture effect. This can cause us to go through life suffering from cumulative damage to our bodies, minds, and spirits without being clear on where it came from!

When we create a habit of pausing, just briefly, before each choice, each *yes*, and each commitment to ask ourselves, "Is this choice in alignment with my heart's true desires for my best life?"—and then allow ourselves to be guided by the answer we receive—everything changes.

That afternoon, when I was considering all the areas to which this simple, mindful practice of checking in with our true desires can apply, it occurred to me that this concept could be easily laser focused and applied to the foods we choose, how we nourish ourselves, and the things we do that support or detract from our health. A love-centered way of eating and nurturing our bodies and spirits based on self-love, desire, self-compassion, and mindfulness empowers us to be the best we can be. It's a powerful tool—and lifestyle—that can give us the authority to let go of our struggles when making choices and habits that affect our health. A Love-Centered Diet sounds inviting, right?

When we connect the dots between the results we'll get from the choice we're about to make with the bigger picture of our deepest desires for our lives, suddenly making the very best, most incredible choices becomes much easier. The things we thought we wanted and were tempted to impulsively consume become the last things we crave. And the things that will actually support our true desires begin to shine brightly and call for us to reach for them more often. Some even taste better! Seriously, the idea of kale used to seem too "blah" to me, but I love it now. I even crave it! Six years ago, if you'd told me I'd be craving foods like kale salad and green smoothies, I'd have rolled on the floor laughing.

The beautiful thing is that there are no extremes here. It's not about being perfect. There really aren't any rules. It's not about counting calories or carbs. It's simply about shifting to live from a place of heightened awareness and following the whisper of your heart to make higher-quality choices that align with the big picture of what you truly desire for your life.

This heightened awareness around your nutrition and health not only includes having more physical energy, being at a healthier weight, and feeling your best, but it also involves a balance of things that add to your joy and sense of pleasure. So on occasion, a few bites of that crazy-delicious-looking dessert or extra vanilla latte might just qualify as aligning with your heart's desire, as long as it's not overdone. When you're tuned in, your heart will always tell you where the balance is.

That same afternoon, I decided to try the Love-Centered Diet and create the habit of always checking in with myself before eating, drinking, or making other lifestyle choices that would impact my health. I needed a practice to add to my happiness foundation that would help me easily stay on track in this area, and something told me this was it. It's simple and full of positivity—and I'm a huge fan of both!

I've always struggled with food choices. Although it became dramatically better for me when I changed my life for the happier several years back, I still struggled a bit with staying on a healthy track consistently, and definitely still had a hard time keeping sugar to a minimum (cupcakes will get me almost every time). An annoying extra eight pounds also tends to sneak on when I go for long periods without paying much attention to my choices (like during the holiday season—ugh!). But that's just it; this happens when I go for *long periods without paying much attention to my choices.* Lack of attention to choices is the root of so much mayhem! Reducing instances of lower-quality choices by training myself to thoughtfully check in with my inner voice before each one has helped me create major positive change in this area (and keep that eight pounds away).

Along with heightening awareness of my food choices to be sure they were in line with my desires for my best life, I added in two more elements of physical health where I knew more awareness and higher-quality choices would make a big difference. First, I wanted to begin moving my body more in general. All the writing and online work I do can easily keep me from moving most of the day if I let it, which is a major health- and energy-zapper, and that's no good. Basically, my goal was just to be more conscious of opportunities to fit in frequent, small slivers of exercise in addition to what I was already getting through yoga and hiking—just stepping it up a bit.

I decided to have a little fun with this goal. So I started dancing while brushing my teeth in the morning (love this one!), choosing to always take the stairs, running around my backyard with my dogs for ten minutes in the afternoon (super-fun), power walking with a girlfriend on a Sunday morning, and other little gems that feel great and could easily fit into my life.

The second was increasing my hydration. I'll talk about this more shortly, but basically I can't emphasize enough how important proper hydration is to our overall health, happiness, and energy level.

When I made these small shifts, I began to see immediate, big results. I not only lost that irritating eight pounds and felt better overall, I also felt hugely energized from taking back complete power over my choices, both small and large. I felt a new sense of control and peace—a more enlightened way of being when it comes to nutrition, health, and overall approach to the everyday.

I've since created a new habit of aligning my choices across all areas of my life with my heart's deepest desires. It took a couple months of very conscious effort before it came naturally, but once it did . . . what a difference. I allow myself the freedom to not be absolute about it all the time (I believe that being just a little reckless on occasion is part of a happy life), but I'm consistent enough to have seen a major positive impact in my life, and I feel a beautiful energy of living in alignment with my truth.

My Mother's Love-Centered Diet

I've watched my amazing mom struggle with food, health issues, and weight my entire life. Her struggle has caused her much frustration and heartache over the years. It's also been heartbreaking for me on many occasions, because when you love someone, you want that person to be happy and healthy.

It all started in her midtwenties, when a number of health issues, along with physical changes from having kids, catapulted her into what would be a decades-long battle.

I remember a time several years back when my mom was looking unwell, frail, and just generally not well. I felt completely freaked out about the state she was in and feared I might lose her within the next few years, which was an unbearable thought. I knew her doctor had recently told her she was in danger and had to make some changes. I called her one night to tell her how I was feeling. I cried and begged her to make drastic changes to turn her health around.

She knew when I called that I was right, and she did begin to take action. Since then, she's lost enough weight to significantly reduce her risk of major health issues, and she exercises regularly—amazing stuff. She looks and feels better than she has in years. But she still finds it difficult to keep the weight off and regularly feels frustrated. Back when I made that call to her, there was so much loving intention behind it, and it did make a difference, but the one thing I didn't have to offer then was a specific tool that would give her a solid place to start. But with the Love-Centered Diet, that was about to change.

I was so passionate and enthusiastic about the changes I'd made through this new lifestyle, I called my mom to share what I'd been doing. I wanted to see what she thought about a diet concept based on self-love and honoring our true big-picture desires. She was the perfect person to ask, since she's basically seen, heard, and tried just about everything.

A self-help skeptic, my mom has tried dozens of diets and lifestyle programs over the years, but she'd never tried (or even heard of) anything with this kind of solid mind-body connection, or anything linking higher thoughts to food choices, which is where I believe true success (and health) lives.

I explained to her what I'd been doing and the positive change I'd created in this area, and she was intrigued enough to try it. I suggested that before each food choice she should consciously ask herself if the snack/meal/drink she's considering is in alignment with her heart's true desires for her best life, and then listen to her inner voice and choose based on the answers she receives. I also asked her to work toward creating a higher awareness in general around how she was taking care of herself. I wanted her to view hydration, rest, and movement as requirements for creating and living her most incredible life. She was already on a good track with exercise, taking part in light-impact group workouts on a regular basis.

Fourteen days after I outlined the Love-Centered Diet for my mom, she called me, elated. "I tried that thing you shared with me, and I've lost seven pounds! It came easily and didn't even feel like a diet . . . more like just making positive choices!" She felt empowered by the new control she'd found that was driven from a more soulful place, and the way it supported her deepest desires for health, energy, and maintaining a healthy weight. It just felt good.

Mark's Love-Centered Diet

A while back, I received a moving e-mail from my old friend Mark that touched my heart. He explained that he'd lacked passion in his life for quite some time and that he felt stuck in a constant quest to find the next activity or big accomplishment that would make him happy and motivate him to take better care of himself. But nothing seemed to be working. "I've tried sports, clubs, philanthropy, mentorships, games, business . . . nothing is resonating," he wrote. "So for the last ten years, I've been going through the motions of life. I have gained close to a hundred pounds in that time, not from fast food or sugary sodas, but from not participating in life."

Not participating in life. Those words stung a bit and echoed in my head for quite a while after reading his e-mail. I can remember times when I also felt completely apathetic toward just about everything. Apathy, if you ask me, is a widespread condition as serious as any other state of emotional distress.

The thing about apathy is that many times it goes unnoticed, because people who are living in a state of apathy aren't necessarily depressed (although it can go hand in hand with depression), and they may not necessarily be unusually stressed or going through any particular hardship. They can simply become disconnected from life, falling into a passive state of going through the motions without much joy, excitement, or drive. They may fall into a place where they believe "that's just the way life is" or that "life's an uphill battle" without realizing so much can actually be done to bring light, ease, and excitement back into their world.

Just as with any other situation we'd like to overcome, the way to begin stepping out of apathy or lack of enthusiasm for life is with action. The Love-Centered Diet is a great place to begin, because it's about mindfully connecting your choices, actions, and self-care to your deepest desires, creating motivation in new ways and igniting greater inner purpose. Radical self-care is an excellent remedy for bringing back mojo.

I scheduled a call with Mark to see how I might be able to help. After he further explained his situation, I shared my mother's story with him and explained the power of the question "Is this choice in alignment with my heart's true desires for my best life?"

I asked him to spend a couple of weeks examining his true desires, making his self-care a priority, and thinking of his choices and actions not just as mundane necessities but as powerful building blocks for the amazing life he was imagining.

By the time we had our next call a couple of weeks later, Mark had empowered himself with some small but significant changes. "There's been a definite shift. I've been drinking more water, eating better in the mornings, and I signed up for tae kwon do classes. This is really a different way to look at things." I'd hoped for some small positive changes, but tae kwon do? How awesome!

"What I realized is that I can't allow my circumstances to run my life," he added. "I feel much more in control of things."

Mark was on an incredible new path to creating new priorities and taking new action based on desire and self-care, rather than just going through every day missing the element of purpose. It wasn't about perfection but instead about love, mindfulness, and sustainable momentum—and therefore brighter days.

Months later, Mark let me know that he was still seeing positive results and continuing to make mindful small changes that were making a difference. He was adding in positive affirmations, cutting back on soda, and even getting excited about planning for his future. Most important, he was beginning to have a renewed vision for possibility in his life.

The Importance of Love-Centered Foods

Another central building block of the Love-Centered Diet enhances it with even more positive energy and impact: The foods we choose should be produced in alignment with love, compassion, and the highest consideration for our health and the health of the planet.

Choosing foods produced organically and humanely, and supporting companies and farms that operate based on these values, raises the positive energy in our lives (and in the world around us), while ensuring our bodies are receiving the highest possible level of love and nutritional quality. This makes consciousness of not only the type of foods we choose but also the *way they are produced*, very important because it's essentially part of ensuring that we stay aligned with our hearts' deepest desires for our best lives.

All of us want to see animals treated humanely and with love, we all want to do our part to preserve the environment, and I don't think any of us really want to munch on pesticides or other disease-causing chemicals. I believe this is quite universal. Aligning these values with what we consume contributes to raising the vibrations of love, kindness, compassion, and positive energy around all we do—essential bricks in our happiness foundation.

I encourage you to look into what's available at your local markets, to do some research and grow your knowledge of food production, food ingredients, and farming practices, and read the labels on the foods you currently buy. Use all the information you empower yourself with to see how you can make some positive shifts to more love-centered foods and raise the quality of the impact you have on the planet as a human. It's not about being perfect or extreme; it's more about making changes in ways that are doable and available to you.

Creating great energy around what we eat supports our physical and spiritual wellness, along with the health and happiness of the planet and all its majestic life. You'll feel great knowing that what you're consuming comes from loving, positive sources, and you'll be supporting farms and businesses that share the same values. It's a high-impact win-win.

Few things elevate happiness levels more than knowing you're making a positive difference in the world, in the lives of others, and in your own life. Choosing love-centered foods is a way to cover all those bases with grace, love, and compassion.

CHOOSING FOODS THAT SUPPORT YOUR HAPPINESS, ENERGY, AND SUCCESS

Choosing foods and creating health practices based on self-love and your big-picture desires for your life is an incredible part of happiness-centered living. Once you create this new habit, the way you look at the foods you enjoy and other supportive elements of your life will permanently shift. When you begin to prioritize your eating and other health-related activities (such as hydration and movement) according to what will support your happiness, energy, and success, positive changes begin immediately and you create a powerful momentum like no other.

You probably have a few super-healthy recipes in your collection that you'd like to make more often. I encourage you to add them to your regular menu. There are so many great resources for healthy recipes: online, books, and even your imagination. Have

The Top Ten Happiness-Boosting Foods

When it comes to choosing foods that boost happiness, an important connection to make is that everything we eat or drink affects our brain or body function in some way. Many foods not only are healthy but also are scientifically shown to support our physiological happiness-boosting systems.

Nutrients such as folate, magnesium, vitamin D, calcium, chromium, and omega-3 fatty acids are all known to elevate mood. Some foods are known to boost serotonin, a natural chemical in your body that balances mood, sleep, memory, and a number of other good things. Healthful foods that are naturally high in mood-lifting nutrients are perfect staples to place at the core of your diet.

Once you zero in on your favorite happiness-boosting foods, it will be easy to reach for them more often. The cool thing is that many of these foods happen to be great tasting, too. I love feeling like I'm indulging a little while eating something super-healthy at the same time. That's a double happiness moment!

Here are ten of the top happiness-boosting foods you can add to your regular menu.

- Almonds (look for dark chocolate–covered almonds for a double happiness lift)
- Avocado
- Baked potatoes (white, such as russet)

fun with it. Make it an adventure. Change up your regular grocery list according to your new priorities, try new foods, and even seek out a new favorite restaurant that serves organic cuisine.

As you add higher-quality foods to your regular menu, also look to phase out things you've been repeating that you know are not in alignment with your best life. Keep in mind that there's a

- Dark chocolate

- Greek yogurt (plain or low in sugar; try with fresh berries for an amazing quick breakfast)

- Leafy greens (especially spinach, kale, or Swiss chard)

- Mushrooms (shiitake, morel, or chanterelle)

- Popcorn

- Roasted pumpkin seeds

- Wild-caught salmon

You can find a free downloadable poster of these happiness foods, along with a few more gifts I've created for you to go with this book, at kristiling.com/operationhappinessresources.

Now that you have a list of happiness-boosting foods to consider, here are a few foods I suggest giving the boot: refined sugar; anything artificial (including coloring and sweeteners); frequent heavy doses of empty carbs (like cereal, pasta, and bread—moderation is okay); all sodas (I love sparkling water flavored with splashes of organic juice instead); processed foods; and . . . anything that generally makes you feel like crap after you eat it. We all have those certain foods we love the taste of but make us feel awful every time we eat them. They're just not worth the loss of energy.

more healthful replacement for just about everything (such as my chocolate ice cream habit that I replaced with dark chocolate–covered almonds), so you don't have to feel deprived if you get creative. I still get my chocolate fix, just in a higher-quality way. The more you consciously and deliberately indulge in things you enjoy that *also* support your health, happiness, and heart's desires, the less you'll crave or even think about the things that don't.

I suggest taking a sheet of paper or your journal and creating a list of foods you love that you know are of high energetic and health value, so you can put them on your shopping list more often and make them part of your routine. In addition to the top ten happiness-boosting foods (pages 128 and 129), here are a few of my favorites that are always on my shopping list.

○ Eggs (I buy organic, free-range eggs when my own backyard chickens aren't laying . . . yes, I raise chickens for eggs and fun—love it!)

○ Frozen organic berries for smoothies (and for using in place of ice to keep drinks cool), especially strawberries (always organic, as nonorganic strawberries are known to contain high levels of pesticides)

○ Granny Smith apples (always organic—these are my secret weapon for banishing belly bloat)

○ Lemons (for cooking and squeezing into water—organic when possible)

○ Pineapple

○ Quinoa

○ Sprouted whole-grain bread

In addition to making high-quality food choices, I take supplements my doctor recommended for me that I feel support my health and energy levels, including a superfoods-based multivitamin, calcium with vitamin D, omega-3s, and a probiotic. To me, supplements are kind of like insurance: We can hope to get all the nutrition we need from our foods, but realistically, that doesn't always work out. Do what feels right for you and share your thoughts with your doctor to get a professional opinion, too. In fact, share all the positive changes you're making with your doctor. It never hurts to affirm these things with people who care, and I guarantee you'll receive enthusiastic support!

Creating Momentum with Morning Food Choices

All meals are important, but breakfast is absolutely your most important meal of the day. *Please. Eat. Breakfast.*

Starting your day by hydrating your body and taking the time to fuel up with nutrient-rich, natural foods is one of the best things you can do in your life to support your happiness, energy levels, and health. It will also help you create positive momentum that will help you stay on track throughout the whole day. Think of it as laying the foundation for a healthy day.

When you're short on time in the morning, or maybe just aren't that hungry yet, it's tempting to put nutrition off until later. Don't. You can't afford it if you're looking to create a fantastic day. When you get up in the morning, your body has gone hours without fuel or hydration. You won't feel like your best self or have the energy you deserve for the day without giving your cells what they need to function at their highest level. You wouldn't try to drive your car with an empty fuel tank, right?

Think about what you're eating in the morning and how you might be able to improve it by reducing sugar and bad fats and eliminating anything processed or artificial. Look to increase plant-based foods and nutritional impact. If you're already choosing pretty healthy options, think of how you can step it up. Remember, what you consume (both nutritionally and energetically) is the fuel of your life.

"Remember, what you consume (both nutritionally and energetically) is the fuel of your life."

QUICK BREAKFAST OPTIONS THAT WILL MAKE YOU FEEL AWESOME

These are just a few super-easy suggestions to help power up your menu. Everyone's different, so you may prefer other options, but I wanted to share some of the healthful ways I nourish my cells (and soul). Have fun discovering what works for you, try new things, and create incredible shifts—not just in the morning but also throughout your day.

○ Raw almonds with a banana or apple (or other grab-and-go fruit)

○ Almond butter or avocado on sprouted-grain bread with a piece of fruit

○ Apple and raw trail mix

○ Smoothie with berries, spinach, water, and organic apple juice (see my favorite go-to smoothie recipe, opposite)

○ Fresh berries with nuts

○ Salad for breakfast (Really, it's the best! My favorites are organic spinach with a hard-boiled egg on top, mixed greens with sliced citrus, or chopped greens with berries. I use balsamic vinaigrette or lemon and olive oil as dressings.)

The Ultimate Energy Drink

A few years ago, when researching the things that have the biggest impact on mood, I learned just how important hydration is to our happiness. Mild dehydration doesn't just affect energy levels; it also affects mood, digestion, vitality, circulation, mental clarity, and so many other crucial areas that can drastically take away from our best life when not functioning at optimal levels. Sluggish physical energy, mental function, and circulation can trigger the blues, irritability, and even depression. Hydration is imperative if we want to be at our happiest and function at our highest level.

Most people are chronically mildly dehydrated and don't even realize it. Did you know that even a 1 percent drop in your body's hydration can reduce your energy level by as much as 10 percent? Ten percent! Nobody wants to spend life running on just 90 percent capacity. Who wants to go through the day with an energy deficit like that? No way! But so many people are doing just that, day after day.

How do you know if you're mildly dehydrated? Well, by the time you feel thirsty, you're already mildly dehydrated (at least 1 percent), because our body's natural thirst sensation doesn't even kick in until then. For many, simply eliminating the chronic dehydration they weren't even aware they had can be life altering. It definitely was for me.

In two 2012 studies (one with healthy men and one with healthy women) conducted at the University of Connecticut's Human Performance Laboratory, researchers found that mild dehydration (about 1.5 percent) caused adverse effects such as fatigue, tension, headaches, and difficulty with mental tasks in both men and

My Happy Fruit and Veggie Smoothie

½ cup wild blueberries (frozen or not)

½ cup organic frozen strawberries

1 banana

1 cup cold-pressed apple juice (organic is best—you can cut sugar by using water in place of juice. I also sometimes use organic carrot juice instead.)

½ to 1 cup water (start with ½ cup and add more, as needed, for desired thickness)

1 handful of organic spinach (blending spinach into a smoothie is a great way to get kids to eat it, too!)

Place all the ingredients into a blender and blend until smooth.

women. The studies also showed that dehydration affects men and women differently. The men experienced more difficulty with mental tasks, especially in the areas of vigilance and working memory. The women experienced more adverse changes in mood and symptoms such as anxiety and fatigue. Basically, drinking enough water can help us all to avoid these issues, feel better, and perform better overall. That's my idea of an energy drink! Drinking enough water does take mindful effort, but the return you get is so worth it. Once you create supportive habits with the goal of staying hydrated, it will come to you with ease.

When I first started my own "Operation Hydration" a few years ago, I created the habit of drinking a glass of water first thing in the morning (extremely important), several glasses throughout the day, and a glass in the evening before bed. I can now really notice a difference in the way I feel if I don't do this. If I go a few hours without water (I try to avoid this, but it happens on occasion), I chug a glass or two as soon as I have the chance. This single change has made an incredibly powerful difference in my life. I feel better, my skin isn't as dry, and my energy level is dramatically improved. And I have little, if any, 3:00 p.m. fatigue!

I now combat almost every icky feeling with water. If I'm blue, fatigued, fighting off a bug, had too much wine, stressed . . . whatever it is, water always fits into the equation.

There are many different opinions out there on what kind of water is best. It's a personal choice, but I go for water produced from a home filtration system. I generally avoid bottled water (not a fan of plastic bottles), and I don't drink tap water unless I'm desperate, although from what I understand, many cities have very high-quality tap water. I also add lemon to my water much of the time, which adds cleansing elements.

Water is the ultimate healer and the very best energy drink. I can't stress hydration enough. It's one of the simplest resources of all to pump up the volume on health and happiness.

Nutrition on the Outside

High-quality nutrition isn't just what we're putting in our bodies; it's what we're putting on and around our bodies, too. Several years ago when I started learning about what's actually in beauty products, personal care products, and cleaning products, two things happened. First, I had to get a handle on my own distress around the fact that some of the stuff is even legal (that's an entire conversation on its own), and second, I made drastic changes to all the products I use, from makeup to cleaning products. There's nothing like being freaked out and grossed out at the same time to inspire rapid, positive change.

Just like with food ingredients and production, I encourage you to protect your health and well-being by examining and learning about the ingredients in the products you use and making shifts that feel right to you. Products produced without harsh chemicals and preservatives but with organic and natural ingredients feel better to use inside and out, and you'll be reducing your risk of everything from chronic allergies to serious disease. Plus, just as you'll find that love-centered foods actually *taste* better, you'll also find that personal-care and home products made with the same loving qualities actually *work* better. I've also found that they come with the cool bonus of a palatable happy energy.

The Environmental Working Group, a nonprofit, nonpartisan organization dedicated to protecting human health and the environment, is a fantastic resource to begin learning about what's in your foods, personal-care products, and other consumer products so you can be empowered with all you need to make more healthful, happy, love-centered choices. Their work in the world is a gift to all of us. You can visit them at ewg.org for some great resources to help you.

YOU ARE EDITOR IN CHIEF OF YOUR LIFE

In writing this book, my desire is to help you permanently infuse more love, self-care, and supportive, positive energy into all areas of your life. I want to help you build a rock-solid foundation for radical, lasting happiness. The Love-Centered Diet mind-set truly fits in with that mission, because the way we eat and take care of our bodies plays a huge role not just in our health but in our happiness as well.

It's really just an uplifting, simple, impactful practice that empowers us to serve as our own guide to our happiest, healthiest life bursting with great energy on all levels. The biggest shift comes from recognizing the link between our food and other choices and the amazing, beautiful bigger picture we imagine for our lives, then using that as motivation to make influential, high-value, self-love-centered decisions.

You are amazingly capable, creative, and powerful. And you are the editor in chief of your life. As editor, always be making choices, creating changes, and moving things around according to what supports your happiness, deepest desires, and ultimately, your most incredible life. It's a joyful, adventurous, evergreen process.

CHAPTER 8

Happy Surroundings: Creating Spaces That Support Your Joy

When you open your eyes in the morning, do you absolutely love the space you're waking up in? Are your bathroom, kitchen, and work spaces set up and designed in ways that help you start your day feeling organized, energized, and together?

Our living spaces can have a significant effect on our happiness, energy, and quality of life. When they're designed and organized in the right way, they can set us up for success on many levels, including sticking to habits that support our happiness and well-being. Sometimes, we don't realize just how much the spaces we're spending time in are affecting the way we feel until we start making changes. Clutter, disorganization, and things we just don't love to look at are like nails in the tires of our joy. And making a few simple changes to create more soulful, uplifting spaces that better support your happiness can make a huge positive difference.

"Clutter, disorganization, and things we just don't love to look at are like nails in the tires of our joy."

MAKING OVER YOUR SACRED SPACES

Because the way we live our mornings is vital to our lives, the spaces in which we spend time before 10:00 a.m. are especially important. So we're going to focus on the bedroom, bathroom, kitchen, and work space as we step into a soulful little adventure in identifying and clearing clutter, embracing a bit of minimalism, and creating inspiring, supportive spaces.

Since many of the principles we'll cover in this chapter can apply to other spaces as well, I encourage you to take any ideas that will work elsewhere and run with them. Think in terms of creating spaces that please and nurture all your senses.

When I began to discover the significant ways our mornings affect the way our lives unfold, it really stood out to me that the design and organization of our living spaces can either hugely support or majorly take away from the quality of our mornings, and our lives. This is especially true when it comes to clutter, one of the biggest joy-zappers, but also when it comes to experiencing beauty (which our souls crave), comfort, inspiration, and breathing space. I closely examined the spaces I was starting my day in. I realized that clutter; old, mismatched linens; a fiasco of an overstuffed closet; a bathroom I didn't like; and disorganized drawers had been draining my good energy and sucking up valuable time, causing me to step into life each day with a slight joy deficit.

After major decluttering, reorganizing, adding some new linens and paint colors, overhauling a closet with the help of a stylish friend, and creating better flow by rearranging some of the furniture, I noticed a huge difference in the way I felt in the mornings, as well as how smoothly my days were going. I felt lighter . . . brighter . . . better. Across the board!

I now schedule a weekend every year to go through and organize, reassess, edit, and redecorate, as needed. I always look forward to that weekend because I know what a difference it will make.

One more thing I did that made a huge difference was hire a

biweekly housekeeper. Confession: Cleaning is not one of my strengths. And to be honest, I just don't like it. I made some small changes and created room in my budget to hire help in this area, and it's been so worth it! If you love cleaning, that's great (I really wish I did). Some people find it meditative. But if you don't, hiring help is well worth the investment. I consider it an important part of self-care. After all, clean spaces are a big joy-booster.

We all have our own ideas about what we can do in our spaces to make them more nurturing, beautiful, and organized, but sometimes life can get in the way. What I'd like to do in this chapter is

Questions to Get You Thinking

Aligning your living spaces with your best life takes effort, but the effort pays off in amazingly powerful ways. As we cover some ideas for adding sparkle to your spaces, keep these questions in mind.

- Does your living environment reflect who you are and what you want?

- Do your bedroom, bathroom, kitchen, and work spaces make you feel peaceful and supported in the best possible ways?

- Are there things in your spaces that drain your energy, such as clothing you never wear, needless clutter, furniture or knick-knacks you don't need or love, or projects you know you're never going to get to?

- When you wake up in the morning, do you feel surrounded by comfort, positive energy, and small reminders that inspire motivation and creativity?

- Are your spaces filled with colors, meaningful objects, and scents that lift you up?

inspire you to link your spaces with your levels of happiness, energy, and success on a daily basis. They are directly connected, and when we recognize this, they become much higher priorities. Our outer world truly does reflect our inner world and vice versa.

You can begin working on three areas that can apply to all your spaces and are also ongoing efforts: Clear spaces of clutter, clear spaces of energy-draining objects, and examine the colors in your spaces to see if you can make changes in paint or other features that will bring a happier feel. Start with these and then apply some of the more specific ideas I share in this chapter that resonate with you, along with any inspiring ideas you come up with.

As you go through this process, keep in mind that these changes don't have to be expensive. In fact, it's worth noting that the biggest positive change will actually come from what you *remove*. There's really something to be said for having less—less to take care of and less to feel enclosed by. You want to own your stuff, not the other way around.

> "There's really something to be said for having less—less to take care of and less to feel enclosed by."

THE INSPIRED BEDROOM

A few simple little things I do for myself make such a difference in the first moments of my day that I'm constantly feeling grateful for these small efforts. I always have a glass of water on my nightstand—without fail. I always keep my robe on the bed at my feet so it's warm and waiting for me the moment I get up. I have my thermostat programmed to come on at 4:00 a.m. to adjust my home to the temperature I like to wake up to. These may sound trivial, but to me, they're reminders that I'm supported and cared for, so I not only benefit from their convenience but from the loving energy they create.

What you keep by your bedside matters. Objects that make you feel peaceful or inspired, contribute to your comfort (such as lip balm), or remind you of the goals you have are great. As I mentioned earlier, I have a favorite framed quote on my nightstand (which I printed out from my computer) along with eyedrops, a candle, and a basket of inspiring books and magazines I love to read. Put some thought into how you might customize your nightstand and bedside to inspire you, lift you up, and make your life a little easier.

Your bedroom is very likely your most sacred personal space. It should radiate peaceful, renewing energy and be free of needless junk. Your bed, sheets, and pillows should be so ridiculously comfortable that it makes you giddy every time you crawl in. You deserve to go to sleep—and wake up—in a place that feels majestic, indulgent, and healthy. Give yourself (and your partner, if you share a bedroom) this gift.

THE BLISSFUL BATHROOM

Let's talk about your bathroom. It's the first room you usually head to after getting up. And we spend way more time in our bathrooms than we realize. Did you know that a person who lives to be seventy-five will spend an average of a year and a half in the bathroom? (For some of us girls, it's probably more like three years!) That's a lot of time to spend in a space you don't absolutely love!

Is your bath decorated in a way that makes you feel uplifted and at peace? I have a canvas hanging in my bathroom that was given to me by a dear friend. It reads, "There is happiness to be found in every moment." That happy reminder is the first thing that greets me when I enter the space. I also keep scented soy candles, my favorite natural soaps, and big piles of fluffy white towels handy. All this sets the tone for the kinds of days I want to create.

Here are a few of my favorite tips for a more inspired, organized bathroom.

- If it's not beautiful or necessary, it goes. (This actually applies to all spaces.)

- If it's expired, it goes. All outdated products are clutter without exception. (Apply this one to your kitchen, too.)

- If it's in your way, out it goes. It can be tempting to cram things into small spaces like bathrooms, but if you're bumping into it or tripping over it, what's the point? Lose it.

- Examine the lighting. Get as much natural light as possible in the morning to energize you, especially in your bathroom. If your bathroom is on the darker side, consider adding a window or a skylight—worthy investments, trust me. High-quality lightbulbs that mimic natural light are also great.

- Consider getting a dimmer. Adding a dimmer to your light switch is an inexpensive way to add a little luxury to the space. This is one of my favorite little improvements to any room in a home.

- Invest in super-comfy, high-quality towels—a must.

When I bought my current house, the bathroom was a real eyesore. It was outdated, dark, and lacked storage. I got creative, and for under two hundred dollars, I transformed it into a beautiful little sanctuary. Paint had a huge impact for the dollar, and hanging a sheer, white shower curtain to let the light in completely brightened it up. I added inexpensive shelves, a light switch dimmer, scented candles, cozy new towels in a wicker basket, a potted orchid—and it was a whole new world in there without draining my energy or my bank account. Gotta love that!

THE KIND KITCHEN

Since we've already covered the core places to begin, and I'm a fan of simplicity, I'll just share with you my favorite easy tips for making your kitchen more supportive of your mornings so you can keep up the momentum with your sacred space makeovers.

Keep in mind that all these points I'm offering aren't rules, just happiness-inspiring ideas and suggestions. Take the ones that vibe with you, add a few of your own, and feel free to ignore the rest. Here are my favorite difference-makers in the kitchen.

○ Wake up prepared. If you're a coffee-drinker, create a new habit of setting your coffeemaker up before you go to bed. This is a little gift you can give to yourself every day. Waking up to the coffee already waiting for you (or when all you have to do is push a button) is a beautiful thing.

○ Switch up your breakfast staples. Take some ideas from Chapter 7 and keep healthy, super-simple breakfast bites on hand so it's as easy as possible for you to reach for things that will energize and nourish your body.

○ Have less stuff. The kitchen tends to be one of the most cluttered spaces in the home. The less you have in there, the less you'll have to clean and maintain, and the more peaceful it will feel. Focus on having fewer dishes, utensils, and knickknacks. In fact, go as minimal as you can bear here. This also makes it much easier to find things when you need them. Get a big box and fill it with items to sell or donate to charity. Anything you don't use, any duplicates, anything you don't like looking at: It all goes.

○ Focus on lighting. Just as in other spaces, lighting is important. If you have dated fluorescent lighting in your kitchen, it's worth the investment to change it out. A dimmer is especially useful in the kitchen so you can avoid being hit with super-bright light early in the mornings.

○ Think bright! Bright colors are uplifting in any space. As beautiful as some dark kitchens look in design magazines, they don't inspire happy feelings or reflect light the way lighter, cooler colors do. When choosing colors for any space, consider first what makes you *feel* good, then go from there.

There's one more thing you can do here that works in all spaces, but especially well in the kitchen. Stand in the center of the room, close your eyes, and let it speak to you. Ask what it needs to inspire and support you, let your soul deliver the answers, and then take action. For me, my soul always calls for lots of natural light, soft fabrics, beautiful plants, and organized storage.

SOULFUL WORK SPACES

Soon after I started making over my mornings, I realized just how important a beautiful, inspiring work space is for overall happiness, energy levels, and success. I'd do all these good things in the morning only to have my great energy slightly deflate as soon as I got into my office, usually before 9:00 a.m. It's not that my office was messy or even unattractive. It was just "blah." There really wasn't anything special to make me feel energized or give me a sense of creative inspiration.

Like my bathroom makeover, my office makeover wasn't expensive or even extensive. I added some cheerful yellow accents, a small altar filled with meaningful objects, some framed photos and quotes, a few plants for a natural element and to clean the air, and a cozy throw to hang on the back of my chair. I also replaced the lightbulbs in my office with full-spectrum bulbs to expand the natural light. The improvement these small changes made was huge and totally worth the effort.

Take a look around your work space and see how you can personalize it, add comfort, and elevate the overall feel. Know which colors energize you and incorporate them with fabrics, paint, pillows, and useful objects. Spending just a day doing this will change how you experience all future days in the space.

Also think about ways you can take a more organized, soulful approach to electronic interaction. Old e-mails, documents, and files on your computer are digital forms of clutter. They're energy-drainers that can secretly zap your motivation, not to mention slow down your computer. Don't save e-mails longer than a week or two, unsubscribe from newsletters you don't read, and review the settings in your e-mail application to see if some small tweaks may help you sort or filter your e-mail with greater ease. And definitely turn off that distracting *ding* sound on your computer that signifies when e-mails come in.

I'm a little embarrassed to share with you that at the time I started making all these great changes to my work space, my inbox contained more than ten thousand old e-mails. Ten thousand! There was junk in there that was three years old. I have no idea how it got to that point or why I had a strange attachment to them, but when I saw the craziness of it, it was easy to let them go and not allow it to happen again.

Finally, remember that a huge percentage of e-mails are from other people wanting something from you. E-mails can be little data-driven soul-suckers. So can text messages and social media messages. While, of course, electronic communication serves a purpose, always know that *your* agenda comes first and align your day that way.

It's so easy to get caught up in the electronic wants and needs of others before taking care of your own goals and desires for the day. Before you know it, it's noon. Don't get pulled into that unproductive cycle. When I get into my office, I take thirty minutes to quickly answer e-mails and check social media. Then I schedule myself an uninterrupted two to three hours to work on my priorities and projects. This helps me use my most valuable time of the day (mornings) on the things that most need my concentration and creative energy (like writing this book). And it feels damn good!

SACRED LITTLE HIDEAWAYS

A quiet, peaceful spot to sit and read, meditate, have a soulful conversation, or just breathe for a few minutes is an important element of self-care and another brick in your happiness foundation. If you ask me, it's a must—especially in the morning when it's vital to consciously set outlook and intentions for the day. Our souls long for it, which is why our hearts swoon a bit when we see images on social media of beautiful bistro tables decorated with lattes and flowers. Stepping away from the places you spend the most time and into a beautiful spot that your mind associates with renewal creates a needed shift that helps you to clear your thoughts and touch base with your inner voice.

You don't need a big area to create your sacred hideaway space. All you need is a simple chair and table under a tree, or a quiet, cozy place in your home where you can chill out and reflect. Even a repurposed closet or the bathroom works in a pinch; just add some mood lighting and stream some soft music on your phone. As long as it gives you the feeling of distraction-free peace for a few minutes, it will work.

I have a friend who has a beautiful potting bench in her garage for planting flowers, crafting, and daydreaming. She takes her tea out there each morning for a couple of minutes to think about how she'd like the day ahead to unfold. It's quiet, inspiring, and fuels her spirit for the day.

Personally, I'm drawn to the outdoors. At my little urban farm in L.A., I've added a healing herb garden, a meditation area, and a cozy seating spot under a giant ash tree in a corner of the property.

The spot under the ash tree is a place where I go just to sit and dream, be creative, and contemplate. It's also the perfect spot to have a cold drink and let my mind wander.

If you don't already have one, how can you create a sacred little getaway spot to dream, rest, and renew? You most likely have everything you need to do this. Identifying and clearing the space, relocating a few objects, and adding a few inspired elements will get you there. Happy dreaming.

CREATING YOUR IMMEDIATE-ACTION LIST

I hope this section on making over your mornings has inspired you to create some radical, soul-inspired changes. Not only will all this action make your mornings and overall life drastically more joyful and successful but it will also create a flow of great reminders that you're taken care of, that you're making yourself and your desires a priority, and that you deserve amazing things.

Mornings are the catalyst for the kind of life we want to live. It's all about starting there with tangible, positive shifts, then taking the practices and tools that work for you and incorporating them into other areas of your days. When you do this, the sun will not just rise and shine brighter on your mornings, it will rise and shine brighter over your entire life. If you're like me, it just may be the biggest thing that will lead you to the happiness breakthroughs you've been longing for. And that, my beautiful, amazing friend, is everything.

LET'S MAKE IT HAPPEN

Use this exercise to create a list of things you can do right away to create positive changes in your mornings. It could be decluttering, changing up your morning menu, adding a daily meditation practice, or a few new habits you'd like to create that you know in your heart will support your happiness.

Ten things I can do right away as a gift to myself to help create outstanding mornings:

1. _____

2. _____

3. _____

4. _____

5. _____

6. _____

7. _____

8. _____

9. _____

10. _____

PART III

CREATE NEW HABITS

+ THIRTY DAYS OF INSIGHT,

LOVE, AND LESSONS

(A Monthlong Daybook)

CHAPTER 9

Eleven Habits of the Happiest People

One of the things I'm passionate about when it comes to happiness is studying the habits, outlooks, and traits that glowingly happy people possess and discovering the ones they seem to have in common. This has taught me so much over the years and has helped me tremendously in creating and sustaining my own happiness, as well as in the work I do to help others do the same.

What I love is that some of the most powerful, supportive habits and traits that have really jumped out at me are not what you'd suspect. Yet they're simple and profound. When you read them, you may be glad to notice you already have some of these habits naturally, and some may pop out as areas you'd like to cultivate while continuing to build your happiness foundation. You may also find that you've started to shift to some of these while reading this book (I hope so!).

Don't feel like you have to be or do all these things at once. I encourage you to really go all out for the habits you feel drawn to or inspired by and then just work to train your mind to incorporate elements of the others into your natural outlook. Developing new habits, retraining your brain, and shifting mind-sets take time and dedication before the magical change happens and they become second nature. It's an ongoing process, and the key is willingness and dedication to doing the work.

ELEVEN HABITS OF THE HAPPIEST PEOPLE

These eleven habits, along with the five key happiness mind-sets outlined in Chapter 2, are core parts of mastering the *skill* of happiness.

#1: Be Deliberately Optimistic

Some people are naturally optimistic. Fortunately for me, I've always been this way. But just because they're natural optimists doesn't mean they always carry a positive attitude. Just like positivity can become a habit, so can negativity. Even naturally optimistic people sometimes have to make an effort to be positive and do it deliberately.

The happiest people know an optimistic outlook is imperative to emotional wellness, quality of life, and even the outcome of some situations. As a result, they put added deliberate effort into being positive and encouraging others to be positive as well. Even if you're not optimistic by nature, you can change that nature by doing the daily work of mindfully shifting to a positive point of view about what each day may bring and any situations that come up in your life. With practice, you'll be more aware of your own negative energy and thoughts as they arise and make immediate shifts until the negativity begins to vanish.

Optimism is not just good for our overall health and happiness; scientific studies show it also plays a strong role in how long we live and in our level of success. Researchers at Yale released a study in 2012 revealing that our genetics account for only 25 percent of the factors that affect how long we live—and we have a significant amount of control over the rest. The study noted that people with positive attitudes live an average of 7.6 years longer than those with a more negative outlook. In another study that same year from Duke University's Fuqua School of Business, 80 percent of CEOs in the United States were labeled by researchers as "very optimistic."

Living with a positive outlook and seeing the best in every situation is something we can *choose*. It's also contagious. When you're optimistic, you will elevate the energy of the people around you, creating a cycle of positivity that lifts everyone up.

Here's an exercise to try that may be a bit challenging but also very helpful. Try getting real with yourself for a few minutes and write down a few things you tend to be negative about that could use a shift in perspective. We all have those things that can trigger us to be negative, but changing the way we view and react to them can make a big difference. For example, I used to be pretty negative about doing my taxes. I'd avoid the task as long as I could because I felt overwhelmed by the amount of paperwork involved and feared writing the check at the end of it. I realized I was making it much more difficult than it needed to be with my negativity, so I focused on changing my perspective. I now see doing my taxes as a sort of annual review of my financial health and look at it as an opportunity to see where improvement and growth can take place. I now actually look forward to the process of getting them done.

#2: Prioritize Mindfully

Happy people have trained themselves to align their choices, intentions, and actions with the highest priorities of love, happiness, and health. They put joy, love, health, and passion first; the rest follows. They dismiss what's unimportant, and they largely ignore trivial minutiae. They keep an inner flow of mind-sets and priorities that positively support them (while saying no to what's out of alignment). Happy people focus on what is wholly aligned with the life they truly desire and freely let the rest fall away without guilt.

This includes regularly examining and spotting even small joy drains they might be tolerating in their lives, and quickly making edits. With awareness, you can train your mind to do this, and you'll notice yourself not caring or being bothered by the little stuff that used to annoy the hell out of you, because your thoughts and energy are way too valuable to be spent on those things any longer. Your attention is incredibly valuable; give it only to what deserves it, and let the rest float away.

I used to allow things like long lines, rude drivers, insensitive posts on social media, and bad service to put a serious wrinkle in my day. Now I barely notice them, and when I do, I dismiss them without much thought and go back to focusing on things that are beneficial to me and to the world. We're in charge of what we focus on and what we respond to, which is incredibly powerful when it comes to happiness.

I do admit: The ridiculous traffic where I live in Los Angeles still frustrates me sometimes, but when I'm stuck in it, I work to make the best of it by listening to an audiobook or calling an old friend. As soon as I make that shift, I stop minding it. We can't control everything, but we can choose and control our thoughts and reactions and prioritize accordingly, which is life changing.

With mindful prioritizing, you'll also be empowered to make better decisions on a daily basis by starting with intentions and turning them into action—and this applies to both the little stuff and the big stuff. This is the path to becoming much more focused on what supports your happiness and well-being rather than being caught up in a cycle of making choices based on other people's agendas.

I didn't used to be this way. I basically went through three decades of my life with pretty scattered priorities. I was a total people-pleaser, and my decisions and actions regularly reflected what others wanted or needed, or what they thought I should be doing rather than what was best for me. Of course, I knew I wanted to be happy, healthy, and loving, but I rarely made strong enough connections in my mind between those desires and most of the choices I was making. This resulted in some regrettable decisions, much unhappiness, and a few unfortunate mistakes.

There's a great meme going around on the Internet that says, "I chose the road less traveled. Now, where the hell am I?" That was completely me back in the day. I was so concerned about helping everyone else with the path they were on that I was rarely connected with my own path. I hardly ever set intentions before taking action, which took so much power away from what I was doing. I still love to take random dirt roads in life quite often, but I do my best to always know exactly where I am, and I always make sure the path I'm on is mine.

> "I still love to take random dirt roads in life quite often, but I do my best to always know exactly where I am, and I always make sure the path I'm on is mine."

Your top priorities in life should be your health and happiness and making sure everything you do and every choice you make comes from a place of love. If you do this, everything else falls into place. Life becomes much easier and more peaceful. Every thought or action you have should somehow, in some way, circle back to one of those three fundamental priorities.

#3: Keep Resources on Hand to Create an Instant Uplift

Happy people are highly aware of the specific things that lift them up, and they naturally and frequently use them when they need a physical and/or emotional boost. Everyone's different, but we all have those little spirit-lifters that instantly make us feel lighter, happier, and more energized. These resources cost very little or nothing at all and don't take a ton of effort, but they provide noticeable results. It's all about creating the habit of reaching for them much more often.

Becoming abundantly conscious of a few of those little go-to things that lift you up and bring you joy, and deliberately incorporating them into your days, can elevate your happiness level across the board. It does take effort to create this habit, because it's so easy to ignore the little stuff that brings us joy when we get busy or feel crappy. But this is when we need them most.

I encourage you to create your own list of a few easy things that never fail to give you an instant mood or energy lift. Then begin to work them into your life as little happiness habits. Create a regular cycle of small, happy items and experiences that can be a standard part of your daily routine (not just occasionally), as well as be there for you when you need an extra boost.

To help you get started, I thought I'd share a few from my own list. This is little stuff, for the most part, but when I became aware a few years ago of how important the little stuff really is to our overall happiness, I started making a conscious effort to include them in my life very regularly. Now anytime I need it (or for no reason at all), I'll go to the checklist in my mind, pick something, and take action.

A few random things from my list: green smoothies, mani-pedis, solo dance party to at least one Flo Rida, Beyoncé, or Rolling Stones song (I can't lie—sometimes this involves being naked just out of the shower), planting or pruning plants in my garden, standing out in the sunshine and breathing in fresh air, fresh flowers, a huge glass of cold water with lemon, a yoga class, texting happy images or words of appreciation to dear friends, a hot bath, poetry, reading great posts on my favorite blogs.

Ready? Grab a pen and create your own list. You can also use a separate piece of paper or your journal. Try to memorize the list if you can, then make these things into mini-priorities. See if you can come up with at least ten, and if you can think of more, even better.

My Go-To Uplift List

1._____

2._____

3._____

4._____

5._____

6._____

7._____

8._____

9._____

10._____

#4: Put Yourself First

The word *selfish* is unfairly vilified. The truth is, sometimes being a bit selfish is actually the best thing we can do for the people we care about. The happiest people frequently tune in to their own needs—without hesitation—and make their own happiness a top priority, which then helps them bring their absolute A game to the people and projects in their lives.

> *"The truth is, sometimes being a bit selfish is actually the best thing we can do for the people we care about."*

Some of today's greatest entrepreneurs are fantastic examples of how putting our own needs and passions first can actually help us be better, do better, and be of much higher service to the world. *They know that happiness fuels success rather than the other way around.*

Richard Branson (once again) is a perfect illustration. He's vocal about making happiness a priority and incorporates his passions into his everyday work life. He has mindfully designed an amazing life for himself that supports him in being the best he can be. He's so in tune with the idea of self-care as a vital part of productivity that his companies offer employees perks such as flexible hours, opportunities to work from home, fitness programs, and fresh fruits and salads on-site free of charge. He encourages his employees to make their needs a top priority—and it benefits everyone!

Fashion designer Diane von Furstenberg is another great example. (And her beautiful designs are on my list of little things that lift me up.) She finds joy and passion in her work; makes business decisions based on what her inner voice tells her; views self-care as a priority; and incorporates elements of self-confidence, empowerment, and service to the world in both her brand and her life—all of which have contributed to her success and to the happiness she radiates.

I've attended many business lectures for executives and entrepreneurs where I've heard time and again how important it is to spend as much time as possible on revenue-generating activities. To that I say, the happiest, most successful people know self-care actually *is* a revenue-generating activity.

If you were taking radical, incredible care of yourself more of the time (i.e., putting yourself first), how would the way you show up in the world change? Think about how your life, certain relationships, and parts of your work might improve dramatically.

When taking care of yourself first, you're also taking care of everyone else who matters in the process, and knowing this will make it so much easier to focus on. Radical, loving, enthusiastic care of your body, mind, and spirit should always be number one. It's the way to be your most incredible self on every level.

#5: Be a Prolific Seeker

In the same way a bee buzzes around seeking pollen from flowers, the happiest people resourcefully seek beauty, joy, adventure, pleasure, growth, and powerful meaning in all areas of life. They're constantly in search of opportunities to marvel, even at the smallest things, and they view life as a classroom packed with lessons and chances to flourish emotionally and spiritually. They drink it all in. This is a quality that can be cultivated and practiced until it becomes second nature, and it's a major part of overall happiness.

There's a little bit of this quality in all of us. But the goal is to let it become a dominant part of who we are and what motivates us. In fact, the seeker in all of us, if not fed on a regular basis, can begin to starve and drive us into emotional crisis. All souls have a great need to be fed with beauty, love, and enlightenment.

To nourish and grow the seeker within you, try these simple exercises that will help awaken your inner seeker and train your mind to always look for light and wonder.

○ In the room you're in now, take a few minutes to look around at the everyday objects surrounding you. Examine each one through the lens of curiosity, amazement, and gratitude. Think about the people involved in bringing those simple objects to the world—the designers, the sales teams, the entrepreneurs. When you think about just how many people put their hearts and expertise into a simple candleholder, ceiling fan, or chair, these little things suddenly become miracles. Begin to look at everything in the world this way, from the smallest objects to the tallest buildings. This way of looking at objects around you will make beautiful things like visual art, music, and nature seem even more magical and amazing.

○ Always look for meaning and ways to grow. Lessons are every-where if we choose to see them. From dreams we have at night to challenging situations we face, there are messages through-out. Seek them out and let them fill your heart with wisdom and appreciation.

○ Seek adventure in absolutely everything. Truly. Even a trip to the porta-potty at the fair can be an adventure (well, that one is probably guaranteed). Looking at every day and every experi-ence as an adventure adds an enchanting thrill to life that can't be explained. Adopt childlike senses of curiosity and wonder. Viewing life as a perpetual adventure can organically fill your heart with awe and infinite gratitude. Not just for the great times, but even for the failures and rotten days. Now, that's awe-some energy to vibe with!

Finally, prolific seekers also find so much more synchronicity in life, because they're on the lookout for it. Let yourself reflect on some of the most amazing coincidences of your life and just marvel at them. They really are mind-blowing! Then think about some of the smaller ones. Even some that may have happened today. Keep an eye out. Connections and links between different things in your life can be beautiful, joy-inducing guides if you let them.

Be a prolific seeker. Approach each day on constant watch for love, fun, wonder, beauty, and magic. All that's amazing is already yours—if you're looking through the right lens.

#6: Don't Make Things Personal

Here's a fact that can be hard to accept, but when we do, it's life changing. Ready? Absolutely nothing others say or do is about you. Ever.

Isn't that a huge relief when you really think about it? Here's the thing. It's their stuff. When others talk about you, do things you feel are against you, or try to wrap you up in unnecessary drama, it has nothing to do with you and everything to do with their own interests and junk. By resisting the temptation to make things about us, we increase our own happiness and peace while at the same time finding more compassion and understanding for the plights and motives of others. The happiest people have the habit of going straight to this inner knowing that it's not about them anytime a relevant situation comes up.

> *"Absolutely nothing others say or do is about you. Ever."*

Even when people offer us constructive suggestions on how we can do something differently, it's still not about us. Rather it's about their genuine desire to be of help and share their own knowledge.

Unfortunately, we do live in a world where some people feel the need to tear down others in order to feel bigger, and because they feel calling attention to the perceived faults of others helps to camouflage their own darkness. Scrolling through social media feeds can demonstrate this clearly. Some are also willing to criticize or throw others under the bus to avoid awkward situations or to evade taking responsibility for mistakes. Some just commit innocent missteps by misdirecting their own pain, self-doubt, or frustration at others.

It's all ego driven, and when we can *know in our hearts that none of it is about us*, we can save ourselves a huge amount of angst. With this view, we can rise above the petty stuff, let much of it go, and, when needed, respond with positivity and love rather than from a place of emotional injury.

This is not to say that you should keep people who treat you poorly in your life. Quite the opposite. Forgive them, understand that this is about them and not you, send them love, and then set the appropriate boundaries.

In addition to not taking personally anything that happens in our lives as a result of others, we need to create the habit of not making things personal about other people. As human beings, we can sometimes fall into the traps of gossip, criticism, comparing ourselves to others, and judgment. By becoming aware of our own tendencies to take part in these low-quality activities, we can redirect that energy to much more productive places. I still catch myself falling into some of these traps now and then, and when I do, I'm able to switch perspective quickly. It's so much better to spend that energy on creating growth and positive vibes, right?

When you take a step back and look deeply at situations where you've been hurt or offended, you'll see that it wasn't really about you. Empower yourself to release hurt and resentment caused by things in the past that were never about you and to easily see new situations for what they truly are.

Speak, act, receive, and perceive from a place of love and compassion, and many of the things that used to seem negative or personal will transform into opportunities for progress, forgiveness, and illumination.

#7: Examine the Worst That Can Happen

Yes, at first this sounds negative, but here's a thought: We tend to think that the "worst that can happen" in many situations is much worse than it actually is. This can cause us to make decisions based on fear instead of reality. In many situations, if we really take a moment to ask ourselves, "What's the worst that can happen here?" the honest answer we receive will be much different from the scenario we were tempted to base decisions on.

> *"We tend to think that the 'worst that can happen' in many situations is much worse than it actually is. This can cause us to make decisions based on fear instead of reality."*

The happiest people know how powerful a careful examination of consequences can be. This can offer an entirely new perspective that can change many outcomes and greatly assist us in making more empowering decisions.

One of the areas where I find this practice very helpful is with obligations that have become unproductive or draining. If I ask myself, "What's the worst that will happen if I gracefully bow out?" the answer usually helps me realize that releasing myself from the obligation is nowhere near as big of a deal as my fear of disappointing people was making it out to be. It takes a ton of pressure off of you.

This can also be very empowering in building the courage to go after our dreams. By taking the time to really examine the reality of the "worst that can happen" if we take that chance, we discover that the outcome isn't nearly bad as our fear is tricking us into believing it is. And this can create space for incredible new doors to fly open. When we know we can absolutely handle the "worst," if by small chance it does become the result, we realize we have much less to lose than we thought we did.

Many of the limitations we're placing on ourselves aren't real— they're illusions. And the habit of taking the time to examine "the worst that can happen" when making decisions or going after our dreams can bring us to an incredible place of fearlessness, peace, and personal power.

#8: Practice Loving-Kindness

It sounds simple, but consistently practicing loving-kindness is not as easy as it sounds. Of course, we make an effort to be kind and loving toward others, but the pressures and distractions of daily life can sometimes take energy from that focus. Consistently acting from an illuminated kindness mind-set takes deliberate, conscious effort but, when done consistently, becomes a habit that changes the vibration of our lives and the lives of those around us. Plus it just feels great.

The happiest, most successful people are in the habit of allowing kindness to be one of the driving forces behind much of what they do in the world. After all, few things amp up happiness like the feeling of doing something kind for another being, human or animal.

A while back, I found an injured songbird in my garden. I was pretty sure it had flown into a window. When it didn't fly away after a few minutes, I was faced with the question of what to do. I was in the middle of a pretty busy workday, and although it was far from convenient, helping the bird automatically became the priority. I scooped it up into a box and Googled local wildlife rescue centers. The closest one was a forty-five-minute drive. Ugh. Off I went.

> *"The happiest, most successful people are in the habit of allowing kindness to be one of the driving forces behind much of what they do in the world."*

As I was driving away after dropping the bird off at the rescue, I was suddenly overcome with emotion. No accomplishment I could have made that day would have meant as much to my heart as helping that little bird. I imagined what the world would be like if that kind of energy prevailed everywhere.

Incorporating higher levels of loving-kindness in our lives not only makes us happier, it can also help us live longer. In 2013, a study at the University of North Carolina at Chapel Hill concluded that increased loving-kindness in our lives actually has a positive effect on our biology, including our nervous system and heart health.

We can train our minds to look out for opportunities to spread kindness. They can be as small as spreading smiles and genuine compliments to people you meet or as significant as volunteering at a local charity. The more we spot and jump on these opportunities, the more we will infuse our world with the energy of loving-kindness.

You can also increase your kindness energy with a loving-kindness meditation. This is becoming an increasingly popular form of meditation, for both its simplicity and its positive impact.

To try a very simple loving-kindness meditation, sit in a quiet place and close your eyes. Breathe deeply and envision yourself and all other beings experiencing infinite happiness, health, love, and peace. Allow the feeling of sending and receiving the loving-kindness energy to flow all around and within you. Do this for at least three minutes and as long as twenty minutes. You'll be amazed by how you'll feel and where this will put your mind. It's a great little practice to incorporate into your mornings, when you feel stressed, or before you go to bed.

Focus on expanding the energy of loving-kindness in your life, and you'll expand the way you *experience* your life in beautiful ways.

#9: Be Aware of Your Energy

Someone with a lot of time on their hands could probably find amusement in counting the number of times I use the word *energy* in this book. There's a great reason for this. Energy is everything.

For much of my life, I was habitually unaware of just how much the energy of those around me, and the energy I was personally carrying, was affecting my life and my happiness.

If I could tell you just one thing that I believe would absolutely bring you more happiness, it would be to *create the habit of being highly aware of the energy you're carrying and emitting into the world around you*. Also, be careful of what kind of energy you allow others to bring into your space (steer clear of negative or heavy energy as much as possible). This also goes for energy created by television, social media, and your surroundings. Tune in frequently, evaluate, and examine the quality of the energy within and around you, noticing what needs to be adjusted or abandoned, then shift accordingly. A great way to begin creating this habit is to regularly ask yourself, "How is my energy right now?" or "Is the energy within and around me the best it can be right now?"

We are very intuitive and energetically sensitive beings. The vibes in our space can affect our joy and energy the same way a dimmer on a light switch can change the brightness of a bulb. You get to decide on the quality of the energy you create and allow into your life, which is huge.

Realizing how drastically energy impacts our lives is tremendously powerful, and when we really get it, we can use it to our advantage. We can filter out what's weighing us down and let more light in. We can share more of our own light with the world and be the dynamic, joyful, full-of-life person we're meant to be.

Upgrade your energy and change your life. Don't you love the simplicity in that?

#10: Let Life Move You

French author and philosopher Albert Camus once said, "Live to the point of tears." The happiest people stay so open to the beauty of life, they receive rushes of awe and complete wonder on a regular basis on multiple levels. They're always finding adventure and opportunities to marvel. They truly absorb and deliberately contemplate the everyday miracles in everything—and yes, more frequently allow majestic beauty and experiences to move them to tears.

Tears can be wonderful. We typically associate them with sorrow, but there are also tears of joy, compassion, relief, and gratitude. When was the last time you can remember shedding tears other than tears of sorrow? Opening up and allowing the kinds of emotions to emanate from within that can inspire the levels of positive emotions that move us to tears is a skill worth practicing.

It was only about two years ago that I shed tears of gratitude for the first time. I was leaving a meeting with some wonderful long-time clients who are true blessings in my life. I was feeling especially open to receiving good things on that day, and their kindness and support toward me always touches me. I got on the freeway to head home and out of nowhere started to cry. For a moment, it confused me because, although I was feeling happy, these were not simply tears of joy. In my mind I asked *Where is* this *coming from?* Then the answer came. Gratitude. I felt an overwhelming sense of gratitude for all the friendship, support, and collaboration these amazing people bring to my life. Since that day, I've allowed gratitude to move me to tears several times. It tends to do that when you really immerse yourself in it.

Give yourself permission to *experience all things more deeply and fully*, to allow passion to live in everything you feel, and to be perpetually amazed and moved by life. It's a beautiful way of being.

#11: Be Aware of the Media You're Consuming

A couple of years ago, I noticed a significant drop in my overall positive energy, and it wasn't hard to figure out where it was coming from. My world was way too saturated with media. E-mail, social media, hundreds of TV channels, the Internet, voicemails, junk snail mail, text messages, instant messages, and more. It all was driving my brain and spirit into information overload, not to mention squashing my productivity and draining my inner peace.

I also felt a sense of loss within my heart. Loss of the calm, open space that lived in my mind before most of this media existed. The space that used to leave room for more wonder, joy, and healthy emptiness was now filled with e-everything. I truly missed that space. I was mourning it. I had to make a shift for my own well-being (and sanity).

I began to tune into this issue and found that I wasn't the only one feeling that way. I took note that some of the happy, successful people I admired were setting major boundaries around the media in their lives.

So I began to create some boundaries around the media in my own life. I spoke to many friends and coaching clients who were all craving change in this area. I realized that in today's information-packed world, where we're constantly bombarded with some form of media (much of it negative) from every direction and every device, it's time for a larger conversation about how this is affecting our happiness, peace, and health.

Social media is here to stay, as is the idea of literally millions of choices of what to watch, listen to, and read. Negativity, violence, an exhausting overload of hyped-up news, and offensive click-bait headlines are everywhere, draining our naturally positive energy. It's all creating a perpetual game of Whack-A-Mole inside our heads. Our minds *must* have room to wander to stay healthy and vibrant. We're literally losing our ability to allow our minds to simply wander freely for more than a few seconds at a time.

We must begin to adapt and change our habits in this area. We have to be more vigilant than ever about mindfully choosing media that lifts us up and contributes to our highest quality of life, while at the same time filtering out much of the negative.

The happiest people today are becoming very good at this. They've consciously cut back and created filters to manage the media in their lives, and even use it to their advantage by adjusting their e-mails and newsfeeds to contain more positive and less negative.

To help you start thinking about what might work for you, here are a few things I did (and regularly stay on top of) to create helpful shifts in this area.

○ **Take time to get your e-mail systems under control.** As we discussed earlier, unsubscribe from newsletters you don't ever open and delete old e-mails. Go into your settings to make adjustments such as automatically emptying deleted items daily, filtering certain e-mails into special folders, and optimizing your spam filters. Turn off any sound that alerts you to new e-mail (a major distraction). Then make an effort to check e-mail less frequently.

○ **Unclutter your social media the way you'd clean out your closet.** Block, hide, or unfollow people or pages with negative, annoying, or spammy posts. Then add a few pages with positive, uplifting posts that will add actual value to your feeds.

○ **Clean up your junk snail mail.** You can do this by calling and unsubscribing to paper catalogs, switching to paperless billing, and even by calling the major credit bureaus to set your credit report to private so you won't get paper spam from credit card companies. You can also speak to your postal carrier about how you can opt out of the junk circulars.

○ **Spend some time thinking about other ways you can adjust the media in your life.** Identify what's draining you and what's lifting you up and regularly make tweaks.

○ **Set your TV to record more shows that lift you up and add to your happiness and growth so they're there when you want them.** Personally, I love most anything home design, health, or garden related, and I also record a number of spiritual shows.

○ **Let go of shows you can live without that are full of negativity or violence.** You won't miss them, trust me. I stopped watching mindless murder dramas, along with most TV news (with the exception of a few morning news shows, since they tend to be light-hearted and sometimes fun). Don't get me wrong, I'm a fan of a good scary movie or historical fiction drama now and then, but I watch these very selectively and in small doses.

○ **Create space for good things.** The whole idea here is to filter out most of the lower-vibe media that's not bettering your life, so you can make room for your mind to wander again and so you can create space for media that will actually support your joy and peace rather than take away from it.

Once you've made strides filtering and reorganizing all your media, you'll have room to begin selectively allowing back in some of the good stuff. Set out to create a new habit of reading or listening to something inspiring and positive each day. It can be short—an uplifting blog, a few pages from a book, a funny or enlightening podcast. Whatever you feel drawn to.

Mornings are ideal for this, but before bed works, too. The idea is to set the tone for more positive energy and a better-quality contribution to your life from the media you're consuming. I now start or end my day with at least one positive, spirit-lifting read, and that habit has made a major difference for me. In fact, it was my inspiration for including the monthlong daybook of essays beginning on page 175. It's my way of offering an immediate (and cool!) resource to help you start creating this habit right away without having to think about where to begin.

SMALL SHIFTS, BIG RESULTS

Our habits are truly the foundation of our happiness and of so many other aspects of our lives. Even the smallest negative habits have impact, while tiny positive habits can have big results. I encourage you to take stock of all your habits and begin making some changes that will support your happiness, wellness, and heart's desires. Know that this isn't an overnight thing. It can take weeks or even months to dissolve old habits and create new ones. Be kind to yourself on this journey, and be willing to cut yourself a lot of breaks. It's not about perfection, just positive change. And it won't always be easy, but it will definitely be worth it.

To make it easier for you to start adopting some new happiness habits and mind-sets, I've created a chart (below) with some random examples of switches you can start with. It highlights how simple some of these habits and mind-set shifts can be. You can also take this chart and use its format as a guide to come up with ideas for your own personal goals for habits you'd like to create.

DO THIS	NOT THAT
First drink of the day: Water	First drink of the day: Coffee
In bed by 11:00 p.m., up by 7:00 a.m.	In bed by midnight, up by 6:00 a.m.
Get up fifteen minutes early for extra time in the a.m.	Hit the snooze button

DO THIS	NOT THAT
Check e-mail or social media after you're up and cared for	Check e-mail before you go to the bathroom (it had to be said)
Look for the love and best traits in others	Criticize
Make your happiness and self-care a top priority	Allow busyness to result in self-neglect
Simplify	Overcomplicate
Read food labels and know what you're eating	Believe hype on packaging
Know everyone needs love and has difficult challenges you're unaware of	Judge
Focus your energy on what you do want	Focus your energy on what you don't want
Check in with your heart's desire before making choices	Make choices offhandedly
Think of happiness as a skill to be practiced daily	Seek happiness externally

THAT'S A WRAP . . . FOR NOW

As we near the end of this wild happiness ride together, keep in mind that you are one of a kind and so is your journey. I've shared some of my stories, struggles, lessons, and solutions, and I'm full of hope that a few have touched you and inspired you to make permanent shifts and additions to the foundation of your happiest life. *Operation Happiness* is by far the longest love letter I've ever written, and I thank you so much for being here and allowing me to share with you, grow with you, and create more happiness with you. Before we wrap it up and move on to the daybook I've put together for you, I have just a few final thoughts to share with you.

Have you ever put much thought into the metamorphosis of a butterfly? I've always been fascinated with it. The caterpillar, after living a pretty dang full life as a caterpillar, sheds its skin for the last time, allowing the new skin underneath to form into a chrysalis, or outer shell. Within the chrysalis, the body of the caterpillar completely transforms, forming new feet, antennae, its own internal GPS, a totally new digestive system, and of course, wings. When it's ready, the butterfly emerges into the world, ready to begin anew. It's mind-blowing! It really is a great example of a miracle and an absolutely perfect metaphor for the many transformations we go through in our own lives.

As you move forward into your mission to master the skill of happiness and build your own happiness foundation using the ideas, practices, and habits in this book (and perhaps a few you'll discover on your own along the way), be totally open and willing to be the caterpillar. Let go of the old stuff, release attachments to anything that's hindering your health and joy, and allow yourself to form new, fresh ideas about what happiness actually is. Be willing to start from a fresh, completely innovative place—to shed your old skin and learn new ways of living. When you do this, you'll grow beautiful wings that will take you wherever you want to go.

In all my research and all the work I've done within myself to finally become a happy person, the biggest thing I've come to realize, next to happiness being an actual *skill*, is that this is all a *way of living* that we choose over and over again, every moment of every day. And knowing that we're a permanent work in progress when it comes to living our happiest lives takes some of the pressure off. It's a mindful and deliberate effort, and we must practice *constantly*.

Life loves you—truly loves you. Life itself won't ever try to rob you of your joy and peace, but some people and circumstances will.

Know they are powerless without your permission. Embrace and focus consciously on your greatness, your loving energy, and your light. When you do this, those things that aren't supporting your highest-quality life will fall away with ease.

Embody love, kindness, compassion, and forgiveness. Become them. Remember that anything can happen . . . *anything.* You are a sparkling light in this universe, connected to all things, deserving of all the love, freedom, peace, and happiness you can imagine. Create it. Be it. Do it. Live it. It's all within your reach, and it's all free. Some amazing, radical, happy adventures are waiting for you as you begin your own Operation Happiness.

Thirty Days of Insight, Love, and Lessons for a Happy Life

Since I began writing articles and blogging several years ago, I've been asked a number of times if I am planning to take them all and put them into a book. I liked the idea of writing a book, but I wanted it to be more than just a collection of essays. So when I began writing *Operation Happiness*, it hit me that offering a collection of my favorite essays as a part of the book would be the perfect way to do this—and it would be just the right way to provide great support in creating the new habit of reading something positive every day.

I've carefully chosen thirty of my favorite essays, articles, and posts from the past few years and included them for you here, to create a month's worth of daily reading. Many of these are very meaningful to me, and many were also my readers' most liked and shared posts. They tell stories, share lessons, and discuss some big questions. (A few of them are behind-the-scenes peeks at some of the lessons I've shared in this book, unfolding in my life as they happened.) I hope you enjoy reading them as much as I've enjoyed writing them. Storytelling is one of my passions, and this is the frosting.

Love & radical happiness,
Kristi

Day 1
Could Thinking Like a Rattlesnake Help You Make Better Choices?

A while back, I was hiking with my dogs when they both simultaneously dove their faces into a bush on the side of the trail. They were a few yards ahead of me, tails wagging with enthusiasm as they looked to satisfy their curiosity. As I approached, I shouted, "Leave it," a command that normally gets them to back away instantly, even from super-tempting treats. But they stayed put, sniffing away.

Thinking it was a rabbit or other furry critter that had scurried under the bush, I walked up and pulled both dogs away by their collars. Peeking into the bush to see what was so interesting, I was shocked to see a nervous, coiled rattlesnake staring back at me piercingly. It was seriously annoyed. It rattled as if to make sure I knew it was not happy and wasn't afraid to strike, but for some reason, it didn't.

I stood there, listening to its rattle, both stunned and supremely awestruck that it had resisted the urge to bite one of the dogs that had been inches from its face. It was a major close call. It held its gaze for a few moments and then calmly took the opportunity to slip away. It must have been aggravated, scared, and unsure of what might occur. Yet somehow it remained composed and discerning. Had the snake been hastier in those moments, it would have been a very bad day for all involved.

I couldn't stop thinking about it. Why on earth didn't the snake strike? I called my brother, who happens to be a well-known expert on reptiles. I told him what had happened and that I was mystified by the fact that both dogs, who were in the snake's face for several long seconds, had escaped unscathed. He explained that a rattlesnake is inclined to hold on to its venom until it is absolutely positive there is no other choice but to use it. This conserves precious energy and resources the snake may need to catch prey. So the rattlesnake remains calm and aware, observing the situation and following its instinct, being exceptionally careful not to allow fear, anger, or assumptions to take over. In this case, no one was hurt, and the snake was able to go find his next meal.

I was fascinated. It makes such perfect sense. I thought, what if we applied this mindful logic when presented with important decisions or facing a conflict? What if we could by instinct remain calm and rational, hold off on making a move until we truly understand all sides of a situation, and then take the time to move forward with the best possible solution? Could thinking like a rattlesnake help us more carefully consider consequences and make better choices that are in line with our best interest?

> *"Could thinking like a rattlesnake help us more carefully consider consequences and make better choices that are in line with our best interest?"*

A great example of where this would apply is when we're tempted to lash out and say or do something we don't mean (and will regret soon after). When this happens, we miss out on creating love, progress, and solutions through peaceful and more productive means. Words and actions brought on by misunderstandings, judgment, and anger are venomous to our lives and our relationships. It all leads to emotional pain and damage that could be avoided with a more objective, thoughtful approach to challenging situations.

The place to begin creating a shift is in truly knowing and being honest with yourself. Learn to recognize, understand, and acknowledge the emotional triggers that make you feel angry, pressured, or fearful when faced with a challenge or decision. Once you're raw and honest with yourself about these triggers, you can teach yourself to stay calm, objective, and peaceful as you move forward.

I know I'll be keeping this approach in mind when considering new projects. I remember a time when I would jump on almost any interesting project that came my way without examining whether it was right for me or would add too much to my plate. Taking the time to assess each new situation and make an educated, conscious decision will honor my time and creative energy.

Where can you be more like the rattlesnake? Small shifts based on this idea can create positive change and make a great difference for you and the people in your life. It's about being true to yourself, keeping your cool, and owning your power. It's about pausing mindfully before moving forward with purpose. And in the end, it's about making love-based choices that use your energy wisely and empower you.

Day 2
Take That Risk—Sometimes the Grass IS Greener Over There

Taking risks, as frightening as some may seem, is a necessary part of a full, happy life. This is what Helen Keller was referring to when she said "Life is either a daring adventure or nothing at all."

Since this idea is a key truth in living our best life, why are so many of us afraid to take the risks that our hearts are nudging us to take? The answer could lie in the need to rethink all the limiting beliefs that resulted from many of our childhood experiences.

Growing up, we heard all kinds of clichéd sayings and "stay small" ideas that eventually conditioned us to create these limiting beliefs, as well as develop the tendency to quiet our own voices. Many of us were taught not to take risks and, in many ways, not speak our minds.

Remember those old ones, "No swimming after eating" and "Children should be seen and not heard"? Total nonsense, right? What about the notions of how dare we think we're awesome? How dare we think we're amazingly talented at something? How dare we "show off" or "brag" about it!

I remember when I was a school-age child, I was so afraid of other kids (and even adults) calling me "stuck up," "show-off," or worse for simply believing I was good at something or wanting to show what I was capable of, that after a while I started to actually believe I wasn't good at those things—I had no right to "show off." So I purposely stayed quiet and careful not to love myself too much or believe I was really good at something.

This mind-set stayed with me into adulthood, until I finally realized through self-reflection and spiritual teachings what total and complete malarkey those limiting beliefs and fears are! I wasn't doing anyone any good (especially myself) by holding back, staying small, and crouching within my comfort zone.

I worked hard to let go of those old beliefs, shift my thoughts, and create big, positive changes. Our purpose is to be happy, to shine, and to share our gifts with the world with love and enthusiasm.

To shine as bright as we're meant to shine, and to live our dreams, we need to be willing to venture outside of our safe space and take risks. We need to release fears about what others will think or say and let go of the fear of change, because holding back doesn't serve us or the world.

> *"To shine as bright as we're meant to shine, and to live our dreams, we need to be willing to venture outside of our safe space and take risks."*

Another old "stay small" saying we commonly hear is "Well, you might want to rethink that one, because the grass always looks greener on the other side!" Translation: Don't take that risk, because the idea that things might get better if you make a change is an illusion.

Now, I am a big believer that the grass we're standing on gets greener when we water it. Sometimes giving more of ourselves in a given situation, or *watering our own grass*, can make all the difference. However, the truth is that sometimes the grass is actually greener on the other side, and sometimes it's time to break free, spread our wings, and go after a change.

Twelve years ago, I made a daring decision to leave a corporate movie studio job that was draining my light and negatively affecting my health. That job was a safe place to be, technically, since the pay was pretty good and the benefits were, too. But the environment there was turbulent, I was always walking on eggshells, and my creativity and talents were basically being kept in a dusty box on a shelf. I had nothing else lined up, no savings to speak of, and I was emotionally bankrupt. But I simply took the leap and trusted the universe that I would land in a much better place.

After a couple of months of healing and rest, I felt called to start my own business and have never looked back! Today, I work from my home studio on my beautiful little city farm, doing work that brings me great joy and allows me to be of service to others. Without ignoring those who were telling me to play it safe by staying in that unhappy situation, and without following what my inner voice was telling me—that the grass just might be greener somewhere else—I wouldn't be living the empowered, happy life I am today. I'm so grateful!

We've been conditioned to feel we're wrong or misguided when we dare to think the grass is greener *over there*, but the truth is, sometimes it IS! If your heart is nagging you to make a change, go for it! Listen to your inner voice. Follow what that whisper is telling you.

There are no mistakes in taking risks. There are only opportunities for growth and learning. In fact, we stay stuck and hold ourselves back from our most powerful, meaningful lives by not being willing to sail out of the safe harbor and pursue the change we desire, come what may.

So, if your inner voice has been telling you it's time for a change, to pursue that dream, to leave that relationship, to move on from that energy-draining job, to move to that new beautiful place . . . do it! You have the power within yourself to move forward to new, greener pastures. Take the risk! Share your gifts with the world. Be happy. Sometimes the grass is greener in that other place. Our hearts always tell us when it is. The magic is created when we make the daring journey.

Day 3
It's Not the Thing You Want—It's the Feeling!

A couple of years ago, I went on a huge, amazing journey to downsize my life. I sold my large house and about 70 percent of everything I owned. I bought a small house on roughly a quarter of an acre and started a little urban farm. I can't tell you how healing, inspiring, and fulfilling it's been.

Along my path to simplicity and minimalism (still working on these, but have made huge progress), I learned a profound, empowering lesson that applies to so many areas.

When it comes to that thing we desire, whether it's a piece of clothing, shoes, or a new job . . . most times, at the end of the day, it's not the *thing* we're truly after but the *feeling* we will have when we get it.

It's all about how we want to *feel* not necessarily what we want to have. (Not that a new job, sweater, car, or pair of shoes isn't awesome now and then.) It's just that many times we find ourselves unfulfilled when we finally get that *thing*, so we buy more things or go after another job, or relationship, or whatever we're drawn to. This can leave us buried under way too much stuff or unsatisfied with a job or relationship we already have because we think we need a new one to be able to feel the way we want to feel.

> *"The key here to authentic joy and lasting fulfillment is to go after the feelings rather than the things."*

The key here to authentic joy and lasting fulfillment is to go after the feelings rather than the things. To learn to create them from within. To look for ways to manifest those feelings of joy and satisfaction with what we already have, both from within ourselves and with our current situations or material possessions.

Begin by focusing on the awesomeness of what is and allowing feelings of tremendous gratitude to flow, even for the small stuff. Make it a regular practice to look around at all that's in your life and say to yourself, "This is freakin' incredible!" Allow yourself to really *feel it*.

When you begin to focus on the *feelings*, two magical things will happen. First, you'll feel a more sustainable state of joy because you're living from a place of gratitude, recognizing the incredible abundance and gifts already present. Everything from material stuff to relationships will become more satisfying and amazing to you. (Yes, please!)

Second, your consciousness will have an automatic filter that will allow you to be more aware when you're making decisions about purchases or major changes. You can ask yourself, "Is it the thing I really want, or am I just looking for the feelings I think may come with it?" If the answer is the feelings, you can look inward for ways to create those feelings without making the major purchase or change. You may even realize you didn't really want that thing in the first place.

This approach will not only help you have fewer possessions and keep you from making life changes based on temporary circumstances but it will also make the things you do purchase and the shifts you do choose to make that much more meaningful and mindful. You'll end up with possessions and circumstances that you're totally in love with. And you won't have a bunch of stuff cluttering your life that just isn't that important to you. How awesome is that?

Focusing on the feeling you're looking for is also great motivation. For example, if you're working on a big project you really want to complete, but you're feeling a little uninspired and overwhelmed by the steps it will take to finish it, try closing your eyes and allowing yourself to feel the feelings of having completed it. Picture the goal accomplished and feel the fireworks of satisfaction going off in your heart. Talk about inspiration to get moving!

This year, I plan to incorporate these practices into my efforts to continue this joyful, simple, amazing life I'm living. I'm grateful for all of it.

Take a look around you right now and see the magic and light that is already in your life. *Can you feel it?*

Day 4
What If You Don't Have to Let Go Completely?

Recently, I found myself in the middle of a kitchen remodel. You can probably relate to the craziness that goes on when you have no kitchen for three weeks. Last week, I had the chance to learn how to use a tile saw. Yep—both scary and awesome at the same time!

I was cutting tiles for the kitchen floor and having a rough time about halfway through because my hands really started to ache and the tiles were chipping on some of the cuts, which was so fantastically frustrating.

About to give up, I tried one more tile, but this time, I decided to see what would happen if I didn't hold on to it so hard when guiding it through the saw.

It was perfect.

Not only did my hands immediately stop hurting, the saw moved through the tile with ease as I guided it and made an absolutely flawless cut. I was so excited! I rocked it! It's the little things, right?

Only this wasn't so little. I finished cutting the tile, and a voice popped into my head and said, "What would happen if you lightened up your grip in some other areas of your life?"

Whoa! It then occurred to me that holding on to some things too tightly had been a pattern in my life for a long time. Struggling to hold on to things that may not want me to keep holding on so tight. Gripping too tightly to things that weren't meant to be exactly the way I wanted them to be. Being too attached to things that just needed a little time and space to manifest into what I was looking to create.

It got me thinking about the idea of letting go—about how letting go is actually often the best way to hold on. But sometimes, that's easier said than done in the moment, especially if we just don't feel ready or if we don't quite have all the answers.

Maybe we don't always have to completely let go of what we're not quite ready to let go of. Maybe, in some situations, we're not meant to let go completely—only just enough to allow space for things to fall together. Sometimes, we can first try just loosening our grip . . . and waiting to see what happens.

> *"Maybe, in some situations, we're not meant to let go completely—only just enough to allow space for things to fall together."*

This could be an amazing way to get unstuck. To change the dynamic of a painful situation, or even to attract something you've been going after but unable to quite make happen. It can allow space to gain insight and see more clearly. It could also be a powerful stepping-stone toward truly letting go, if that's what's meant to be.

What comes to my mind in a big way is a past relationship. I did everything I could, in the most loving way I could muster at the time, to save it from ending. But the more I held on and tightened my grip, the farther out the ship sailed and the more things fell apart. Holding on so tightly only made things worse and didn't offer the chance or space for things to come around naturally. Looking back, the most powerful, healing, and loving way to fight for what I believed in would have been to lighten my grip. To let go a little. Just like with the tile saw.

So what could change if you lightened your grip? Didn't hold on so feverishly? Created the space for a particular situation to naturally blossom or change, and allowed things to happen in their own time? Empowered yourself to move forward whether or not you're totally "over it" yet?

It just might be the beautiful, amazing middle ground you've been looking for.

Day 5
How a Journey to Have Less Helped Heal My Heart

In the spring of 2013, I made a huge decision to drastically downsize my life. My ten-year marriage had come to a heart-wrenching end months before, and that January, having just made it through my first holiday season in eleven years without my husband, I found myself living alone in a very large house, surrounded by silence and a decade's worth of accumulated possessions. I didn't know where I was going from there, and, at times, it felt like I didn't have the energy to care. My heart was broken, and for the first time in my life, I had no plan.

I remember standing in the middle of the living room feeling overwhelmed by all the responsibility I was facing in the wake of what I'd been through. Sometimes, putting your life back together actually begins with taking everything apart.

> "*Sometimes, putting your life back together actually begins with taking everything apart.*"

In that moment there in the living room, I suddenly felt very clear about what I needed to do next. I wanted to downsize—not just a little, but drastically. I wanted to sell the big stucco house with no yard and find a small home with a garden. I wanted to travel. To simplify. To live freely.

I then realized the beautiful future that could be waiting for me was currently buried under a ton of stuff. So I went on a crusade to sell, donate, or give away as much as I could. My goal was to lose 70 percent of it. It was a big challenge, but it felt completely empowering. Once I began my mission, the doors that started to fly open for me blew me away. The house sold in forty-eight hours for more than the asking price. The perfect home for me appeared—a tiny house surrounded by trees on nearly a quarter-acre alongside the Los Angeles River, and my offer was accepted over eighteen others. Help was coming to me from every direction in unexpected forms. I knew in my heart that the universe had my back, and I felt supported.

With every step in my downsizing journey, my heart was healing, and at the same time opening again. The steps I'd been taking to lighten my load and take charge of my life, along with the healing work I'd been doing internally, opened me to the possibility of a new relationship, new ways of living, new friend-ships, and other new opportunities from a place of wholeness instead of lack, which made all the difference.

After escrow closed on my old home, I said a teary goodbye that was both emotional and cathartic and put the remainder of my possessions into storage (all but a single suitcase). I had thirty days until I could move into my new home. What to do!? I'd taken the month off work, had no stuff and no place to be. I was a free bird, and it felt pretty amazing.

I went to stay on a foldout couch at the home of some of my best friends. We all lived in community for a month, sharing stories and meals by the pool, laughing, crying, dreaming, and making plans. I could feel and see the color and light coming back into my world. And you know what? I didn't miss the stuff.

Not one single thing, not for one moment. I didn't even think about it, and it was truly eye-opening. I had a truckload of possessions hidden away in storage, and for weeks, I'd forgotten any of it even existed.

When I moved into my new home, I was very selective about what I brought with me. Half of what had been in storage didn't make the cut. I spent time writing and working in the garden and decided to turn the property into a small, sustainable urban farm. I added vegetable beds and a chicken coop and brought the neglected fruit trees back to life. As the land flourished, my spirit did, too.

It seemed that what I needed kept appearing at just the right time. I finally felt ready to begin putting energy back into serving through my writing, speaking, and coaching again, and I was amazed by how my experiences had empowered me to be stronger in every area.

The lessons that came from that time will fuel me for as long as I'm around. I thought moving on from my old life and into a new one would be one of the hardest things I would ever have to do, and it was. But what I wasn't expecting was that it would also be one of the most enlightening journeys I've ever made. I learned that simplicity, love, authentic forgiveness, vulnerability, and minimalism are the keys to creating a truly free life filled with light. I learned that getting really clear about what you want often starts with getting really clear about what you don't want.

This morning, in the middle of writing this article, my eleven-year-old German shepherd, Venus, escaped the yard after the gardener accidentally left the gate open. After several minutes of frantic searching, I found her a few blocks away sniffing around, happily trotting and wagging her tail, making new friends. Relieved, I bent down and put my arms around her. I looked her in the eyes, and I could see a spark of bubbling joy. I realized that in those few minutes of wild abandon, she probably felt much the way I did during those healing days of freedom by the pool with my beloved tribe.

Instead of being angry with Venus for going out on her little adventure, I scratched her on the head with an understanding touch, and she followed me home. I was grateful to her for reminding me that few things in life are more valuable than living freely and being *willing* to allow ourselves to heal and grow by stepping out of what we've always known to explore uncharted waters.

Day 6
Go Ahead and Feel Free to Wander

In case you've been wondering, it's okay to be a wanderer. It's okay to not know what you want to be when you grow up—no matter what your age. It's okay to deliberately create totally new chapters of your life anytime you feel inspired to explore, to marvel, to desire.

Love everything and everyone; make your art; plant your seeds. Live with amazement, passion, and a sense of wonder. Shake things up. Let go of the tendency to compare yourself to others, and definitely let go of attachment to other people's opinions.

Free yourself from the idea of what you thought your life would be or should be, and be enlivened and spellbound by what is and what can be. You are a radiant, gifted being of light. Embrace the now and be ready and open for what might be next. Go after that dream your heart's been longing for. Wander. Seek adventure. Remember, anything can happen!

"Let go of the tendency to compare yourself to others, and definitely let go of attachment to other people's opinions."

Day 7

How to Destress and Embrace Abundance

Ever catch yourself completely stressed out about something and then have a lightbulb moment and laugh at yourself when you realize how unnecessary (or even silly) the stressful tripping is? Well, I've been in the middle of a kitchen remodel. Not a big fan of the dust and chaos, but so excited for my inspiring new space to create beautiful, healthy food!

I recently had a major wake-up moment and a good laugh at myself when I recognized a specific trap I fell into and saw how easy it was to instantly change my entire outlook and experience with one powerful but simple realization. Love those shifts!

I'd been feeling a bit stressed out about the whole kitchen thing. Other than the expected chaos of sink deliveries, pending construction, and appliance shopping, I was feeling a little crazed about going over budget and all the extra expenses that had been piling up (you know how the old saying about home stuff goes . . . everything takes twice as long and costs twice as much as you plan). I was driving home from shopping for faucets when it hit me: *I'd fallen into the lack trap!*

What's the lack trap? Basically, it's allowing yourself to fall into a mind-set of lack or "not enough" in any given situation, whether it's financially or on another level. When I realized I was viewing the entire project from a place of lack instead of a place of abundance and light, I realized that was exactly why I seemed to be attracting more lack! Ding! I completely cracked myself up with how silly it was, and I immediately felt less stressed and more peaceful about the entire project. Peaceful about a kitchen remodel? Yes, it's possible!

What we focus on expands, and the energy we put out attracts the same energy in return. I wasn't doing myself any service by focusing on the mounting expenses and falling into the mind-set of not enough. Yes, it's absolutely important to be mindful about spending and creating a realistic budget, but it's also important to have the confidence that even if unexpected things pop up (and they usually do), there's always a way to work it out.

The universe is looking out for you, and when you shift your focus and mind-set to abundance and expansion, you support the universe in sending more goodness your way. So that's my big tip to share with you; approach all you do with a mind-set of abundance and having enough. Allow yourself the inner knowing that even when challenges come your way, there is always a way to work things out (even if it's not the exact way you might first envision). This is a great way to keep stress to a minimum and make things happen.

> *"The universe is looking out for you, and when you shift your focus and mind-set to abundance and expansion, you support the universe in sending more goodness your way."*

Here are two more of my favorite ways to reduce stress and more fully enjoy all that is.

1. No matter what you have on your plate, make your self-care a top priority. It's easy to neglect your own needs when things get busy, but we must take care of ourselves in order to show up in our full awesomeness for those who are important to us. Schedule time for the gym, a massage, a bath, or even a few minutes each morning for a quiet cup of tea. This will support you in joyfully gliding through all you have on your calendar.

2. Speaking of calendars, I am very guarded with my calendar. It's easy to let our schedule get too full to live fully, and this is a major energy- and joy-sucker. If I don't schedule myself

regular quiet evenings at home, free time to be creative, and time to just chill out, I see the results showing up everywhere. Also, I am careful about what I say yes to. If it's not "Hell yes!" it's "Hell no!" Funny how this strategy works: You soon will find your calendar 98 percent full of hell yeses, which is an awesome way to live!

Day 8
When Your Heart Says "Hell No!"— How to Step Out of a Bad Situation

So I had a random little experience while visiting Paris (I'm in love with that city) earlier this month that was empowering, a little brave, super-fun, and thought provoking—all at the same time.

My friend and I had booked an afternoon tour to visit Monet's gardens at Giverny, which I was looking forward to, being a passionate gardener. On the day of the tour, it poured rain. I'm talking buckets.

We showed up since the booking confirmation said rain or shine. The bus was an hour late to pick up our group, and the city was gridlocked with traffic jams. We were feeling uneasy about the circumstances but boarded the bus anyway.

A few minutes into the ride, rain pounding so hard we couldn't see out the windows, the driver announced that it would take at least ninety minutes to get to our destination, at which point we might only have half an hour before they closed. I looked around the bus, which was inching along in traffic, and saw people looking pretty miserable. I tapped my friend on the shoulder and whispered, "Do you want to get off? Do you want me to ask the driver to stop the bus?" It was an easy decision.

I got up and politely asked the driver to stop the bus so we could jump off. We had no plan, but anything seemed better than spending four hours round trip on a tour bus to spend thirty minutes at a garden in the middle of a storm.

At the next light, the driver opened the doors, and we said, "Au revoir," jumping off the bus in the rain, laughing and feeling thrilled with our decision. How to spend a free afternoon . . . in Paris . . . in the rain? Suddenly, the rain seemed like the best thing in the world!

We walked the shops and found a little café, where we ordered a bottle of wine, some amazing food, and spent time people watching and chatting with locals. It was a delicious, joy-filled few hours that turned out to be the result of a good, split-second decision to abandon a plan gone wrong.

This experience got me thinking about how many times in our lives we find ourselves on a bus we probably shouldn't have gotten on, headed in a direction we don't feel good about.

We've all been in situations where our inner voices were telling us to abandon ship and, for whatever reason, we kept going to our own detriment. We give in to pressure from obligation, pressure from others, or fear of disappointing people, or maybe even because we invested and are hesitant to lose our investment, even if the price of staying on course is more costly.

We spent more than two hundred dollars on that tour, but we realized quickly that even if we didn't get our money back, it was worth the loss not to have to waste an afternoon stuck in traffic on a tour bus. We weighed our options and decided the potential loss was okay with us—and it turned out to be the right decision.

"If there is any situation in your life—a job, a relationship, an obligation—anything you don't feel right about and have been unsure how to handle or have been afraid to exit . . . just do it."

So here's what I want to share with you and get you thinking about: If there is any situation in your life—a job, a relationship, an obligation—anything you don't feel right about and have been unsure how to handle or have been afraid to exit . . . just do it. It doesn't have to be a graceful exit. It doesn't have to be perfect, and you may disappoint some people. But it's not about that. It's about being true to you.

I can remember times when I stayed unhappy in jobs for way too long, went on trips I didn't want to go on, and gave my time out of obligation to things that didn't feed my soul. I can remember many times I went through with things I didn't want to do because I was afraid of disappointing people.

Now, there is something to be said for keeping a commitment if it's going to hurt people or cause big problems if you don't follow through, but 95 percent of the time, that's not the case. And you want to know what else? People will forgive you, and they're much more understanding than you think.

Many of these situations can be avoided by being more conscious of and really examining how you feel about a commitment or situation before getting yourself embedded in it. Sometimes, a no is the best solution. But they can't always be avoided—sometimes, we don't know things are going to go south until we're in the thick of them.

So if you're in one of these situations, how do you begin your plan to get off your metaphorical bus to misery? First, ask yourself, "What's the worst that can happen?" or "Can they do fine without me, really?" You'll find that the answers are usually pretty supportive of your desire to exit. Trust me, almost every time, they CAN get by without you, and everything will be fine.

Then make a call, have a conversation, or send an e-mail—whatever you feel is appropriate—and kindly explain from your heart the way you feel, that you need to remove yourself, and that, if needed, you are happy to assist with any transition resulting from your exit. It can be uncomfortable, but the discomfort will be short-lived, and the result just may be an amazing afternoon at a Paris café—or something even better.

Let go of what's not working. Be brave enough to move on. Make bold choices. It's okay if they're last minute, split second, or otherwise—as long as you're following your inner voice. Be audacious enough to ask the driver to stop the bus so you can jump off and see what adventures are waiting for you.

Day 9
Is Loving-Kindness the Ultimate Multivitamin?

A while back, I was sitting in the peaceful waiting area at my gym, waiting for a massage appointment. Another woman sat down to my left just as two ladies entered arm in arm, one helping the other into a chair. When I saw their faces, I knew right away they were mother and daughter. The striking resemblance between mothers and daughters (or fathers and sons), physically and in terms of mannerisms, is one of those beautiful wonders in life. What was special about this pair was that the daughter looked to be in her midseventies.

The woman sitting next to me asked them if they were mother and daughter, and the younger woman answered, "Yes, this is my mom. She just turned ninety-four."

I smiled, listening to these sweet ladies converse. The ninety-four-year-old mom said energetically, "Are we all relaxed today, ladies?" She was full of light and joy.

The woman next to me said to her, "You look amazing and full of life! What's your secret?"

Without hesitation, the mom replied, "I've always surrounded myself with nice people. That's the secret."

I was touched by both the power and the simplicity of her answer. I've often thought about, and even written about, how allowing unkind, negative people into our lives can affect our emotional and physical well-being. I'm a big believer in being very mindful about what we tolerate. But I hadn't really thought too much about how it could affect our physical health in the long term, and specifically our longevity, until now.

Could it be that after conscious healthy eating and regular physical activity, the next most powerful key to a long life is kindness? As kindness is an expression of love, and love is the most powerful force known to us, this connection is undeniable. Psychology affects our biology in powerful ways and therefore our longevity.

> *"Could it be that after conscious healthy eating and regular physical activity, the next most powerful key to a long life is kindness?"*

Many studies support this idea, including a 2013 study at the University of North Carolina at Chapel Hill where half the participants were assigned to take part in a loving-kindness meditation each week for six weeks. The other half was assigned to a control group.

Participants in the group taking part in the loving-kindness meditation practice increased in positive emotions in comparison to those in the control group, as well as increased in vagal tone (the activity of the vagus nerve, our longest cranial nerve). In general, the greater the vagal tone, the greater the physical health of the person, especially heart health. The study results suggest that positive emotions of loving-kindness, positive social connections, and physical health influence one another in a self-sustaining, upward-spiral dynamic.

Increased love and kindness in our lives affect our biology in impactful, healthy, and positive ways. This is great news, because it means that we have more tools to increase our physical well-being, as well as our chances for longer, fuller, happier lives.

We can eat healthfully, exercise daily, and even live a relatively happy life. But if toxic, negative people are around us on a consistent basis, and we're allowing their negativity to affect us within—like a slow-moving bacterial infection—this alone could bring on disease by weakening our defenses.

On the flip side, even if the negative energy created by others in our lives is at a very low level, I believe our health and longevity can be affected by being closed off to the abundance of love and kindness offered to us from so many sources. The key here is to make a shift to being mindful—consistently remaining in a state of openness and deliberately noticing the beauty in the world, especially during rough times. This can mean something as small as taking a moment to breathe in and be grateful for a smile from a stranger.

Here are some thoughts on how we can make a shift to reduce the negativity we absorb from others and increase the levels of love and kindness we give and receive.

- The energy we put out comes right back to us. If we begin to take responsibility for it and make a conscious effort to be kinder, gentler, more compassionate, and more loving toward others—on a consistent and meaningful level—the kindness and love that comes back to us to fill our hearts will be greatly magnified and will be a source of light for others. Like attracts like.

- We must look closely at, and be mindful of, what we tolerate. Everyone has ups and downs, but if there are people in your life who are consistently negative, unkind, or toxic, changes need to be made. Walk away from, or decrease your exposure to, those people who drain you in negative ways. You deserve to be treated with love in every scenario.

- Change the way you look at some of the negative people you experience. Know that toxic, negative, hurtful behavior is a cry for love and acceptance. By seeing a person who is being negative or hurtful with compassion and love, we can change the way we respond to that person. Perhaps we can even create a powerful positive shift that will break a toxic cycle (for ourselves and for that person) through our response of love and kindness. This is a great place to start healing relationships.

The message we can receive here is that we have the power to choose to create simple shifts right now, shifts that will benefit both our physical health and emotional fitness (as well as others') in amazingly positive ways and increase our chances of becoming centenarians with ease.

I also believe there is an even greater message here to be considered. The answers science has been looking for to increase the human life span don't necessarily lie with pharmaceuticals, animal studies, or test tubes but may lie in a kinder, more loving, more giving world.

As citizens of this global community, the call to action from this perspective is to collectively work together to shift our energy to love, compassion, and kindness—in purposeful ways on such a level that the duration of our lifetime on this earth can be expanded beyond what we ever thought was possible. Long live loving-kindness.

Day 10
How to Be Happy and Grow Through Dark Times

People often ask me, "How are you so dang happy all the time?!" Well, here's the scoop: I'm not. Well, at least not completely. But I do consider myself a super-happy, fulfilled person overall, which feels awesome and is something I couldn't honestly say ten years ago. Life feels good! I do have challenging days now and then, and even bumpy weeks and months. I go through major storms and general life BS, and all the ups and downs. What I know with certainty is that there is a key to staying happy even when times are hard and when it comes to shifting our whole perspective on creating our happiest life. In fact, it could be the single biggest approach to living our happiest existence.

Being happy is not just about choosing to be happy moment to moment. It's not just in the great days and fabulous occasions. It's about knowing down deep that no matter what's going on, we have the tools, the gratitude, and the love within us to find joy within the dark times, too. To know in our core that the clouds will pass in their own time and that, underneath it all, our happiness is still there to support us, even when we're not feeling it.

In the history of the sky, there has never been a cloud that didn't eventually pass, right? And beyond the clouds, the sky is always bright and blue. So being a happy person is about knowing down deep that our happiness is always there inside us— bright and blue, just like the sky on the other side of the clouds. It's about knowing that no matter what's happening, it's okay to still find moments of joy and great value underneath it all. To be grateful for the good that is. For the lessons. To focus on love. This is how to be happy through the clouds. When we get this, really get it, we can reach in anytime we need it and allow the rays to begin shining through. This is not only the key to making it through dark times more easily, it's also a core path to healing.

The last few years of my life have been by far the most challenging yet. I recovered from a painful, debilitating illness that lasted more than a year, two of my dear lifelong friends passed away suddenly, I lost a mentor who was a true beacon in my life, and my ten-year marriage came to an end. And there was also unpleasant life junk mixed in there to add to the fun (surgeries, moves, you name it).

Yes, there were days I felt like I might just shrivel up like a dried leaf and blow away in the wind. On those days, I just allowed myself to *feel it* (because it's perfectly okay to allow yourself to have days that suck once in a while without beating yourself up about it). On the worst days, I found light by mindfully sending loving energy to those people and situations that were painful for me.

With all this, believe it or not, the past five years have also been the space for some of the happiest times in my life. This is because a few years ago, I finally understood that being happy through—and in spite of—the storms is the answer to a truly happy life. This knowing has been at my core through it all. It's looking for and embracing those moments of joy during even the darkest times that can help us get through. It's having the strength to reach for the smallest spark of light, even when we feel broken open. This is what pulls us through.

> " . . . *I finally understood that being happy through—and in spite of—the storms is the answer to a truly happy life.*"

Allowing ourselves to feel, acknowledge, and process sadness, grief, anger, and all those other feelings is an instrumental part of moving forward and living our happiest lives. All those emotions are valid and help us heal and grow. But during these times, we also tend to create an inner struggle to squash joy, because the ego can make us believe that joy shouldn't exist during those times. The powerful truth is that so much sweet stuff and so many lessons that add to our happiness come to us through these emotions and experiences.

A while back, I cracked open a fortune cookie and the message inside said "The cloud will rain success on you." Times had been rough, but I knew the clouds were beginning to part and thought to myself, "Yep! I'll take that!" The fortune stayed on my refrigerator for days until, after seeing it several times, the true message finally hit me. It's awesome if you think about it. It wasn't saying

"When this crap is over, success will come your way" but rather "The cloud over your head right now is going to rain good stuff on you—WHILE you're under it—so keep your eye out!" Exactly!

The most amazing gifts, lessons, and experiences are sometimes found *under* the clouds. Our job is to stay open, look for moments of joy, receive, and let it rain.

Day 11
Five Keys for Attracting Supportive, Positive People

We're all looking for ways to consistently surround ourselves with a supportive, positive network of people who believe in our dreams and lift us up. Cultivating and nurturing a posse of positive, uplifting, enthusiastic people who have your back is a crucial part of creating your success and joy on all levels.

But how can we expand our network of people who light us up? How do we simplify meeting, getting to know, and staying in contact with our network? Here are five keys to help you get started creating your own superstar empowerment network and attracting a supportive, positive tribe.

1. **Be what you seek.** BE that person who is supportive and positive toward others, and in turn you will attract supportive, positive people into your corner. The energy you project is the energy you will receive in return, so be sure to bring it when you attend social and business events.

2. **Turn off traditional media.** Begin subscribing to positive news and blog posts that make you feel supported and uplifted. Instead of negative news, try watching TED talks, subscribe to uplifting blogs, listen to positive podcasts. This will shift your internal energy and put you in a better place to attract people into your life who are in line with all you wish to create.

3. **Seek out people who are actually DOING.** Look for ways to connect with those who are successfully creating for themselves the energy that you want: career, love, networks of friends, etc. Then don't be afraid to reach out. A great way to begin is to ask if there is a way you can be of help to them. Being of service to others is always a fabulous place to start.

4. **Do what you LOVE.** Find a way to make what you like to do part of your networking. People will be drawn to you when you are living your passions. Find ways to incorporate things you love to do into your everyday work or projects. And reduce the energy you spend on things you don't love (I personally don't love texting, so I try to use it only for quick plan making or to send addresses, phone numbers, etc.). I try instead to communicate by phone, e-mail, or social media.

5. **Carefully choose how you spend your time.** When an invitation doesn't make your soul leap, consider saying no. Your time is valuable, so the more you spend it cultivating relationships and projects that feed your soul, the more empowered you will be. And remember that just because an opportunity seems a bit uncomfortable doesn't mean you should turn it down. Sometimes, stepping outside of your comfort zone is exactly what you need to shake things up in super-positive ways. The best way to attract a network of people who will light you up and inspire you is to be that light for others.

> *"The best way to attract a network of people who will light you up and inspire you is to be that light for others."*

Start with kindness, being of service, and being genuinely interested in the passions of people you connect with. You may even discover some new passions of your own, in addition to amazing, soul-feeding friendships.

Day 12
Is Your Schedule Too Full to Live Fully? Three Ways to Create More Free Time

I've been feeling lately like I need to take a look at my schedule and do some serious unscheduling, which I try to do whenever I hear my inner voice whispering to me to slow down. I've become pretty good at managing this over the years (with a lot of practice), as free time and time for myself are like oxygen to me and to my creativity. I didn't used to be so good at the scheduling stuff, and I still have to be mindful about it or things will creep into my schedule that I have no idea why I said yes to.

Ever look at something coming up on your calendar and think, "How the 'bleep' did THAT happen?" Fortunately for me, working to align my schedule with what makes my heart sing has helped me greatly reduce those moments.

Recently, I was doing some gardening in my little backyard farm in L.A., and it occurred to me that nature has this scheduling and load-lightening stuff down to a science! A great example I took note of was that when a fruit tree feels stressed, lacks nutrients, or has too much young fruit growing on it, it drops some of the fruit before it develops. This allows the tree to focus its energy and resources on the fruit that remains and in turn create beautiful, big, juicy works of art! As I looked at all the unripened little citrus fruits lying on the ground around my orange and grapefruit trees, I felt inspired by this simple concept. Sometimes, we just need to release what's not serving us and drop some fruit!

Back in the day, I would run myself ragged with jam-packed

days, excess travel, and too many projects at once. I'd do all this without considering how much of my energy it was taking until I would find myself depleted and unable to focus on what was actually important to me. It wasn't until several years ago (back in 2008) that I finally hit a wall, physically and emotionally, and knew I had to make some changes. I thought I'd share some of those changes with you here, so you can take what might work for you and apply it to help lighten your schedule and your life.

1. Make it a positive habit to think mindfully about obligations and projects before saying yes to them. If your soul isn't telling you "hell yeah!," then seriously consider a no.

2. Even if you're making an effort to allow only things that feed your soul (or things that are absolutely necessary) on your schedule, sometimes your schedule will still become too full. Make a point each week or month to check in with your calendar and ask yourself, "Is my schedule too full to live fully?" If the answer is yes, look for some things to drop or reschedule for a time when your load is lighter.

3. Schedule unscheduled time. Purposely leave some mornings, afternoons, even entire days blank so you can have some time now and then to just zone out or do something you feel inspired by in those moments. I block out time in my schedule to have absolutely nothing planned, and I always end up thanking myself. Not to mention, some of the best times are the spontaneous ones—when you just go where the wind takes you.

> *"If your soul isn't telling you "hell yeah!,"*
> *then seriously consider a no."*

Think about living more like a fruit tree and learn to tune in to the need to drop some of your fruit so you can recharge and focus on what's important to you. Shift your focus to schedule your life with things that light you up, feed your spirit, and help you feel excited about each and every day. It will take some practice for this to become habit, but if you're open to this change, it will make a major positive difference in the quality of your life.

Day 13
Important Reasons You Need a Vacation Now

The other day I spoke to a friend who told me she hadn't taken a vacation for over three years, and she felt completely burnt out. When I asked her why she'd gone so long without a break, she said she'd been super-busy and never seemed to be able to fit it in. She also explained that in the office where she works, there's a sort of silent discouragement when it comes to taking time off. This made me a little sad and really got me thinking how many people are living that same scenario.

I've learned through my own experience that when it comes to things like rest, travel, or anything else we long for, if we're not making the time, we're making excuses. In our culture here in America, there is a certain pressure overall not to take much time off. A sort of "vacation shaming" exists that is counterproductive on so many levels. We do it to others, to ourselves, and we even do it to the president of the United States every time he picks up a golf club.

We must let go of this old-school idea that taking time off somehow decreases productivity or implies someone is not fully dedicated to his or her work. It's quite the opposite. Taking ample time to rest our body, mind, and spirit increases productivity, amplifies creativity, and even elevates the quality of our work. It's time to ditch outdated mind-sets and embrace balance and flexibility.

I believe a company filled with a bunch of burned-out, low-energy people who rarely take time off makes less money in the long run than if they were to give each of those employees several weeks a year of vacation time and make it mandatory they take it. Happy people make fantastic employees. Some successful companies with smart leadership know this, and they make ample vacation time, work-at-home days, and other soulful perks available for their staff.

When our soul needs rest, we can feel the call. If we ignore that call for too long, we can burn out, lose our mojo, become physically ill, or even drive ourselves into emotional bankruptcy.

If you haven't had a vacation since you took a few days off three years ago to attend your cousin's wedding, you absolutely need a break now. If you haven't taken more than a week off in over a year because you've been "too busy," your schedule is too full to live fully.

Really, it doesn't matter how long it's been. It doesn't even matter if you went to Hawaii for ten days last month. If you're feeling like you need a break, you need one, and you'll be a sharper, more fulfilled, healthier version of yourself for taking it.

Here's the thing. You don't just owe this to yourself. You owe it to those you love. To those you work with. You owe it to the world. Because if you're rested, happy, and well, you can show up as your most incredible, dynamic, energetic self for everyone and everything in your life.

> "If you're rested, happy, and well, you can show up as your most incredible, dynamic, energetic self for everyone and everything in your life"

Allow yourself space in your life for vacations and downtime. Take it without apology. Live. Make this a priority and your life will reach new levels of joy, peace, and success. The busyness can wait.

Day 14
How to Be Responsible for Your Energy and Shine Brighter

Learning to recognize when you need to shift your energy to a higher, brighter vibration is an awesome skill that is worth expanding.

Regularly tune in to ask yourself, "How is my energy right now and is it lifting me up, as well as the people around me?" Then, if needed, take steps toward shifting. You can also ask yourself, "Am I approaching my world and the people in my life with big love right now?"

Choosing to see the world and everything around us through a loving lens is the key to creating a life filled with high-quality energy, joy, and peace. It also offers us effective, conscious approaches to problem solving—especially in relationships.

> "*Choosing to see the world and everything around us through a loving lens is the key to creating a life filled with high-quality energy, joy, and peace.*"

I can think back on several times when simple shifts in the energy I was putting out would have changed the course of my life in positive ways and definitely would have spared me from a few crash-and-burn moments. I take full responsibility for those times now, have learned from them, and clearly see how my low vibrations negatively affected different situations. Focusing on love is where it's at.

Over the past couple of years especially, it's become crystal clear to me that if we can open ourselves to looking in the mirror and seeing when the energy we're carrying is negative or coming from a place of lack, we take back our power to create quantum change. It can be challenging, but with an open mind, heightened awareness, and practice, these kinds of energy self-checks will come naturally and be hugely beneficial.

We can do many things to shift our energy. The key is finding what works for you personally and then keeping those things in your toolbox to pull out and apply, when needed. When your energy changes, you can literally feel it in your core. Here are three ideas I've found helpful for creating personal energy shifts.

1. Change gears and do something different. Go for a walk, spend a few minutes with a pet, hit the gym, or turn on some music and have a two-minute dance party. Or simply take some deep breaths and shift focus on something funny or uplifting.

2. Take a few minutes to sit somewhere in silence and think only about love, compassion, what you're grateful for, and positive intentions.

3. Do something healthy for your cells. Pop a multivitamin, drink a green drink, hydrate your body with a big glass of purified water, have an organic veggie salad for lunch. Doing something healthy for your body will lift you up and create an immediate shift in your energy, both on a physical level and a vibrational one.

Create the habit of regularly turning inward for an energy self-check. When we shine bright, everyone and everything around us shines brighter, too.

Day 15
Time Does Not Heal All Wounds— Here's What Does!

It's been beautiful here in L.A., so I've had tons of opportunities to work in my garden. It's one of those things that totally lights me up!

While building a fence over the weekend (yes, me with hammers, nails, wood, and wire!), I had a powerful thought about happiness, grief, and our ability to heal that I wanted to share with you.

I was happily hammering away at a fence post when I felt familiar pangs of pain yanking at my heart. They came on suddenly, as they sometimes do. I felt a little frustrated that a loss that occurred nearly two years ago was still stabbing at me at the most random moments. Can you relate?

Even the happiest, most grounded people aren't immune to pain from transition, grief, or loss, which everyone will experience at some point. I grew up believing the old saying "Time heals all wounds." I heard it from my family, from the media, and from my teachers. However, I've come to know the real, big truth about that . . . *time itself doesn't heal anything at all—WE DO—it just takes time to do it.*

Truth is, sometimes it takes quite a while, and we need to push on, even when we don't want to—cut ourselves a break for the time it's taking. Continue actively taking steps to heal and move forward. Every single day.

Healing, just like happiness, does not take place without action. Action is what heals. Effort. Practice. It may not be what we want to hear, but it's the truth. And it's where our power to thrive and shine again resides.

"Healing, just like happiness, does not take place without action. Action is what heals."

So what I want to share with you is: if you're hanging out waiting for time to heal your heart, your spirit, or even your body . . . we all need to remember it's not time's responsibility to do that . . . it's ours, and action is required if progress is going to happen. Time is just a friend to help us along the journey.

We heal our heartache, grief, and regret through action, growth, forgiveness, and gratitude through frequent, deliberate steps to move forward and into the awesomeness and light that is right here in this moment and is always waiting for us around the next corner, if we allow it to be.

Have you ever read the book *The Pillars of the Earth* by Ken Follett? It's my favorite novel. It contains a great analogy for this message.

In *The Pillars of the Earth*, it took the builders of twelfth-century England decades to build the massive, majestic cathedrals. Everyone talks about how long it took. But time did not build the cathedrals; the builders did. Their effort, sweat, creativity, and *action* . . . and just look at the amazing result. They powered through and made it happen, no matter what life threw at them.

So I invite you to join me in recognizing that *we are always the ones with the power*. While time is a factor (a broken bone, for example, takes a certain amount of time—but also care—to heal), it's not the driving force.

What healing actions can you take today to expand your happiness and health? Step forward, break out your best moves, and make room for the amazing things that are waiting. Here we go!

Day 16
Are You Living with Hidden Negative Energy?

Recently, on a long flight home over the holidays, I discovered something that really got me thinking. Sometimes, very small, even unnoticed, things we allow in our lives are covertly draining our energy and adding negative vibes to our existence.

> *" Sometimes, very small, even unnoticed, things we allow in our lives are covertly draining our energy and adding negative vibes to our existence. "*

Squished into a tiny window seat on the plane and making the best of it, I had decided to go through and delete numbers and addresses from my phone that I knew weren't good anymore. People that had moved, changed phone numbers, or whatever. I was sure there were at least a handful of them in there.

What I found surprised and even startled me a bit. There were tons of contacts that had no purpose taking up space in my phone, or my life, any longer. Some of them were ten years old. People I'd worked with on a single project a decade ago, a few toxic people I'd distanced myself from years prior, duplicate entries (can you say clutter?), and, I'm embarrassed to admit it, but even a few people I'd put in by first name and had no idea who they were.

What really struck me is that some of the names even packed a little sting when I looked at them. I've let go of many difficult things from the past, so why was I allowing some of them to come calling again via reminders in my address book? I wondered why I'd let all these entries I no longer needed exist in my phone for so long. Part of me wanted to kick myself (*step off, inner mean girl!*), but instead I decided to see it as a lesson.

As minor as it seems, all those unneeded contacts had been like tiny little flashes of negative energy every time I had to scroll through the names in my phone. I wondered where else I was allowing overlooked clutter or negative reminders to detract from my positive energy. I went on a mission to seek and eliminate.

There was more. Much more. In previously ignored piles of papers in my desk drawers (old tax bills and expired coupons), in a filing cabinet in my garage (court documents no longer needed), and even in my jewelry box (lonely single earrings that had been missing the matches for at least a year and were sad to look at). The keyboard for my Mac was screaming to be cleaned. Typing away on a dirty keyboard was definitely not helping my creativity.

I also realized some of the things that had been radiating energy-sucking vibes in my life were actually things I hadn't wanted to let go of before: piles of photos from long-past relationships and old x-rays and medical records from surgeries that happened years ago.

I realized having these things around wasn't serving me in any positive way. On top of that, simply by existing in my personal space, they were quietly draining tiny bits of my positive energy the way a nail slowly drains the air from a tire. It may not happen right away, but eventually the tire goes flat. Or blows.

Since this major lightbulb moment, I've been on a little mission. Each time I come across something that no longer serves me or doesn't in some way add positive energy, I immediately chuck, donate, clean, or shred it. It's an entirely new and deeper level of clutter busting. I've made it part of my self-care practice, and it's been surprisingly empowering.

Where in your life are you tolerating hidden negative energy? Look closely. What you discover might amaze you and leave you scratching your head.

A great athlete looks to eliminate any minuscule thing that drains energy or might hinder performance. We should do the same for ourselves in our everyday lives. Why continue settling for less? Seek, identify, eliminate, and then watch the light in your life shine even brighter.

Day 17
Three Important Truths about Happiness

If you ask ten different people how to achieve happiness, it's very likely you will receive ten different answers. Everyone has different views and thoughts about what makes them happy, and in some ways, it's definitely a uniquely personal journey. However, some universal keys and skills for living a truly happy life can make all the difference.

Personally, I believe happiness should be a subject they teach in school, starting at an early age. It is, after all, one of our most important life skills, if not the most important. Proven methods and techniques for being fundamentally happy can be learned and practiced just like playing the piano. But unfortunately, unlike piano lessons, we don't commonly engage in happiness lessons.

Growing up, we're misled to believe that happiness comes to us through success, material things, relationships, achievements, and other external sources. While these can be wonderful and can contribute to a happy life, they're only building blocks and are not part of the concrete foundation of happiness.

Building a foundation for living a fundamentally happy life takes deliberate effort, knowledge, practice, and habits that support happiness from within, even through dark times.

Like so many, I spent years and years as an achievement junkie, chasing happiness, finding it in small, temporary doses through external sources. While these would bring temporary highs, I would always find myself returning to a basic setting of lack and emotional mediocrity.

It wasn't until my early thirties that I finally realized my strategy wasn't working. I changed course, turned within, and through dedicated practice and work with some wildly inspiring mentors, I discovered how to change my core emotional setting to one of overall happiness and peace. Since then, my life has drastically changed. I no longer go through long periods of darkness, there are more good days because I have learned to create them that way, and I have a much easier time bouncing back from setbacks and hard times.

While there are many elements to building a foundation for lasting happiness, including the practices of mindfulness, gratitude, self-acceptance, and love, three important truths about happiness have stood out to me as things that often go unrecognized but, once understood, can change the way we think about and approach happiness.

The first is that *being sad now and then is actually part of a happy, balanced life*. It's a complete myth that truly happy people never feel depressed, defeated, or distraught. On top of this, we tend to beat ourselves up for having these feelings instead of surrendering and allowing them to flow through. It's about learning to recognize that there are valuable lessons to be learned from any situation and knowing that underneath everything you are guided and loved. It's also about going within and feeling grateful for those opportunities and learning how to deliberately find joy, even in the smallest doses, during the tough situations.

People often ask me how I am so damn happy all the time.

The answer is I'm not, but I have learned to find joy, peace, and lessons within the sad times, which helps me bounce back that much faster.

The second truth is *that being happy is a way of life that takes deliberate hard work, concentration, and practice.* Sometimes, you even have to struggle and fight for it by defending personal boundaries and making hard decisions. The good news is that the more you work at it, the better you get, and it will begin to come naturally. There are happiness "muscles," and the more you work them and keep working them, the stronger they get and the more they will support you. This is a concept I wish I'd come to know much earlier.

You can learn to be happier just like you can learn to play a game of chess. In chess, you learn and develop skills and strategies for setting yourself up for success, deciding exactly what to do when pieces are lost and how to bounce back when the going gets tough. Being happy works very much the same.

Finally, *being happy is much more physical than you would think.* It's true that it comes from within, but everything physical, from what you eat to physical activity to simple acts like cracking a smile, affect energy levels and brain chemistry, directly impacting our levels of happiness. Happiness is not just something we choose, find, or feel, it's something we do.

> *"Happiness is not just something we choose, find, or feel, it's something we do."*

Next time you feel down or anxiety ridden, think *activity.* Start working on a project you've been putting off, get some exercise, meditate, put on some music and do a happy dance, down some ultra-healthy food, even just move around a bit and do some stretching. The results are immediate. Do these things daily and your level of overall happiness will increase drastically.

Take on the challenge of building yourself a solid foundation of happiness practices and skills that will be there to support you in living your happiest life. Ultimately, being happy is a conscious choice we must make on a daily (and sometimes even moment by moment) basis and a skill we must continually practice.

You can absolutely change your internal setting to one that idles regularly on happiness and joy, but it does take effort. Be willing. Make it a project. Start with small changes. Create practices that make you feel happy, keep them up, and don't beat yourself up for not being perfect at it. We're all works in progress, which is part of what makes life a beautiful adventure.

Day 18
Embracing Your Creative Inner Wild Child

When I want to expand my creative mind to help me put the finishing touches on projects I'm working on, get ready for a speaking event, or bust through blocks when I'm writing, I break out colored pencils, paint, and other random art supplies and just set my creative inner wild child free.

Sometimes, when we're feeling a little "meh" or out of touch with spirit, art—or any kind of free creative expression—can be an amazing way *to reconnect with our souls and unleash ideas and passions* that were stuck in the mud.

You don't need to go out and buy fancy art supplies or paint like Picasso. Just grab whatever's around—crayons, pens, sticky notes—and let your inner being guide you.

You can also grab a pen and pad of paper and create fun lists, like "stuff that inspires me in epic ways" or "ten things I want to do this month that are outside my comfort zone."

Just the act of doing something different and giving your inner wild child a chance to speak to you is a "*fanta*-bulous" way to tap back into your light! You can also do something physical—a new kind of yoga class, a trail run, or just dance around your living room (one of my faves).

> *"Just the act of doing something different and giving your inner wild child a chance to speak to you is a 'fanta-bulous' way to tap back into your light!"*

What can you do to tap into your creative side and embrace your inner wild child? Ready? Time for some creative, artistic *fun* . . . one of life's vital nutrients!

Day 19
Three Things to Do When Everything Sucks

Sometimes life doesn't just throw you lemons, it throws you grenades. So . . . what to do on those days and weeks when it seems like everything is crap? How do you stay happy and healthy through it? I use a number of practices and ideas that help me during challenging times, and they make a tremendous difference.

Here's one thing I know for sure: When things don't go your way, there will be another way . . . a better way. It just may not be clear immediately. The key is to trust, stay open, and love yourself through all of it.

> *"When things don't go your way, there will be another way . . . a better way. It just may not be clear immediately. The key is to trust, stay open, and love yourself through all of it."*

Here are three things to try when it seems like everything sucks.

1. **Step into big-time self-care mode.** I'm talking amp it up in major ways! We should always be in self-care and self-love mode, but when things get tough, extra self-care can make a huge difference for your health, happiness, and sanity.

   So don't just schedule one yoga class, massage, or long walk in nature—schedule many! Indulge without guilt. Take a mental health day (trust me, the world will not end if you do this). Take hot baths with salts, call friends who make you laugh, watch a favorite movie with a "*gi*-normous" bowl of your favorite comfort food. Focus your energy on treating yourself like the fabulous rock star you are! This will not only help you release anxiety and bounce back faster, but it will also help you stay strong, positive, and productive through the storm.

2. **Go into super-healthy-eating mode.** What you eat has a tremendous impact on how you feel. It affects your anxiety levels, brain chemistry, happiness meter, and of course your physical and emotional energy. I generally work to eat super-healthy most all the time. I'm all about greens, smoothies, and other healthy goodies. But I'm not always perfect in this area (and that's okay!). However, when times get tough, I really amp up the healthy, clean eating to compensate for the extra stress my mind and body are experiencing. (This also works great when I feel like I'm fighting off a cold bug.) I hit the green juice big time, I make sure not to miss my supplements, and I cut out sugar and double up on the healthy salads and water with lemon. This not only helps me stay healthier through the tough times but it also gives me the great feeling of taking charge of something I *can* control instead of focusing on the stuff I can't.

3. **Step outside of your regular zone. Do something different.** It doesn't have to be anything huge, dramatic, or requiring a ton of effort. Try cooking a new recipe, visiting a local museum,

or hitting a movie solo. One of my favorite easy things to do when I feel blah is to just jump up and dance around the room for a minute or two. Blast some disco on my iPhone and just jump around! I smile the whole time, and within a couple of minutes, I feel like a new person. This also works great for busting afternoon fatigue.

If you're inspired, feel free to make it epic if that's what's calling you! If you have the energy and time, do something totally crazy! Last week, I booked a last-minute trip and spent four days in Hawaii. I literally said "eff it!"—booked it, packed, and went. I brought my laptop so I could work on the trip and had a blast doing it. Hawaii is one of my happy places, and I came back renewed and ready to face what was waiting.

Create a list of additional steps you can follow to take the best possible care of yourself—not just when stress levels boil over, but all the time. Then, when things are tough, kick it up a notch! Get wild. Shake it up and shake it off. Happiness, healing, and success all rely on some kind of action. This is where our power lives.

Day 20
Avoiding Burnout: Seven Ideas for Happier Workdays

We've all been there: that feeling of being overwhelmed and mentally exhausted from ever-growing lists of tasks, messages, and e-mails demanding our energy and attention.

The drive for fifty-hour-plus workweeks, combined with technological advances that keep our mental gears constantly turning, has resulted in millions of overcaffeinated, sleep-deprived, burned-out employees and business owners who dream about moving to an island to work at a seaside mai tai bar.

Many of us can also add several hours a week sitting in traffic to our work schedules.

Through the years of working for myself, I've learned that I'm much stronger and more successful with projects when I'm taking excellent care of my body, mind, and spirit. Finding this sense of harmony took much practice, and I find myself revisiting priorities on a regular basis to keep it up.

All it takes to bring more bliss and success into our professional and personal lives is to tweak our way of thinking and change a few of our own rules. After all, it's usually our own made-up rules that hold us back, not the rules created by others.

It's a given that working less and slowing down to a more peaceful pace at the office can lead you to a happier work life. If you feel like this isn't an option, consider this: Slowing down, taking better care of yourself, and taking regular time off will result in more focus, extra organization, and a significant increase in mental energy. As a result, more productive days and higher-quality work will emerge. So it's a win-win.

Easier said than done? It may seem that way, but even making a few tiny changes can make a huge difference and provide the momentum you need for permanent positive change. Here are a few suggestions.

1. **Resist the temptation to work late unless it's absolutely necessary.** This may take practice, but it's well worth it. Downtime must be a priority so you can be at your best for you, for your career, and for those you work with.

> " . . . even making a few tiny changes can
> make a huge difference and provide
> the momentum you need for permanent
> positive change."

2. **Keep an inspiration box** in your office filled with special notes from friends and loved ones, as well as a few trinkets that remind you of good times. Take a break now and then when you need a pick-me-up and go through the box for instant motivation.

3. **Make a conscious effort to schedule evenings out** after work every few weeks with friendly colleagues or people who inspire you. Laughter is always the best medicine, and brainstorming in a nonwork environment can be motivating as well as valuable.

4. **Change the setting on your e-mail program so it only checks for new messages every thirty minutes.** Your sense of peace will increase dramatically, and you'll get more done without the constant interruptions. While you're at it, turn off the sound notification as well. Who needs extra noise?

5. **Schedule e-mail- and phone-free days on weekends.** Sink into the joys of being unreachable for a few hours. Indulge in news-free days now and then, too.

6. **Check in with yourself** on a regular basis for self-care tune-ups. It can take practice to keep priorities in line.

7. **Take a little time for soul-searching.** If you are truly unhappy with your job and feel this can't be transformed, even if you shake things up a bit, then consider a change. If you feel trapped and a change doesn't seem feasible, sit down and see if you can map out a six-month plan to make it happen. What you come up with might surprise you.

One of the most important secrets to a successful career and happier life overall is whole, balanced living. If your self "scale" is tipped heavily on the side of work, take a big step back and see where you can shave off some of the weight. The payoff will be worth it.

Day 21
You Need a Bliss List

I'm a big fan of lists. I love them. Something about writing things down helps reinforce things in our minds and putting things on paper just makes them a little more . . . electric. At the start of this year, did you create a list of goals or resolutions? I always do. But this year, I realized that most of us are forgetting to create another very important, empowering list: One that can help us stay on track with happiness, stay connected to our inner voices, and help compel us to keep creating our dream lives. *A list of the things that light up our souls.*

Why is this so important? Because it's super-easy to get so focused on achieving goals and routines of everyday life that we forget to deliberately incorporate the things that really light us up, support our happiness, and drive our inspiration. And because spending time turning inward and tapping into our hearts can lead to new discoveries about our passions, what's really important, and how we can better invite the things that truly bring joy into our lives more often.

Anytime we're creating a list of goals, we should also be creating a list of the things that light us up and fill our souls with bliss—a bliss list. You can even compare the two lists to see what connects to what, adding more fuel and clarity to your plan.

> *"Anytime we're creating a list of goals, we should also be creating a list of the things that light us up and fill our souls with bliss—a bliss list."*

Personally, I love lists of ten. I create them all the time. This just seems like a doable number to me. Not overdone or underdone.

But sometimes just listing for as long as the ideas flow can be awesome, too.

To help you get started, I thought I'd share my current list of ten things that light me up right now. They're big and small, simple and complex. And to me, they're all a "Hell yes!"

1. Stand-up paddleboarding

2. Snorkeling and free diving

3. Writing

4. Helping others to think about and approach happiness in new ways

5. Deep, soulful conversations with friends and family

6. Cooking

7. Gardening, fresh flowers, and growing my own food

8. Sunsets

9. Stargazing

10. Great music (especially live)

Grab a pen, find a quiet spot, connect to your heart, and create your list of things that really, truly light up your soul. You might be surprised by what appears on it. *Let your heart speak through your pen.* I suggest handwriting for sure, because it stimulates the brain in ways that help with comprehension and focus. Plus, it's just a soulful break from anything electronic, and we need as many of those as we can get.

Create and re-create this list often. Keep it where you can see it every day. Think of it as a heart-centered meditation, an action plan, and a to-do list all in one. Of all of our lists, *the list of what truly lights us up and fills us with awe is the most powerful and significant.*

Day 22
Why You Must Forgive What You Think You Can't

Healing and true peace begins with forgiveness. Most of us know this deep down, but it can be very challenging to remember and follow through on when we feel wronged or hurt in some way. True forgiveness, whether it's for yourself or someone else, takes strength, compassion, and the willingness to let go. It also takes knowing that the person you're truly setting free is you. It's like a superfood for the soul.

> *"True forgiveness, whether it's for yourself or someone else, takes strength, compassion, and the willingness to let go. It also takes knowing that the person you're truly setting free is you."*

A number of years ago, I was coming out of a bank in Los Angeles with a friend on a sunny, carefree weekday morning when I was attacked violently by a young guy frantic for money to buy drugs. We weren't more than ten feet from the front of the building, walking and chatting away, when I heard footsteps running up behind me. My spine froze. Somehow in that brief moment, I knew what was coming.

Before I could react, something smashed into the side of my head like a brick (actually, we're pretty sure it was *literally* a brick). Everything went dark for a few seconds, and I could hear my friend screaming like the world was ending. I felt my bag being ripped from my shoulder and heard the footsteps again as he ran away. It almost didn't seem real.

Later that day, lying in a cold bed at the hospital, I can clearly remember the thoughts that were present in my mind. I did freak out briefly, but after the initial shock subsided, I felt strangely peaceful and thankful that I'd recover from the injuries, with the exception of a minor hearing loss in my left ear. I had what seemed like endless questions, but mostly I just wanted to know why it happened. I wanted to understand what could bring a person to that kind of lost desperation. It seemed so sad to me.

About a week later, a kind person called to say my bag had been found not far from the bank. I was anxious to go through it to see what had been left behind. There wasn't much. A stack of my business cards, chewing gum, and ironically, a can of pepper spray (a lot of good that did for me). I pulled out one last thing—a library card from the nearby Santa Monica Library, belonging to another young woman. My heart skipped a beat.

I called information, got a number, and called her up. We bonded right away, sharing our experiences. Two different police departments were investigating our cases, and when we put the detectives on our cases in touch, they were able to piece together enough information to track the man down. I felt empowered.

Strangely, what I felt when I went to court and saw him wasn't anger, fear, or resentment. It was empathy and compassion. The aching sadness in the energy that was coming from him was clearly visible. He knew he'd messed up his life in an epic way. He was a handsome guy who had come to L.A. to be an actor, found himself lost, depressed, and tangled in a web of addiction and mistakes. What he did to me had nothing to do with me. It was an act of fear and desperation. Some might think it strange, but a part of me felt sad for him.

After it was all over, people in my life were concerned. They thought I should be emotionally traumatized. Some had me convinced that I might be, or should at least be looking for reasons to be, so I went to a few sessions of therapy to be sure.

I found the therapy sessions unnecessary and even somewhat draining. There was nothing wrong. Nothing I needed to work through. In fact, everything was right. I felt like I'd grown tremendously from the experience. I was more self-aware, had straightened out some priorities, and was grateful for having been given a powerful reminder that every moment is a precious gift. Not just every day, but every single moment.

It wasn't until years later that I came to fully understand that the precise reason I wasn't emotionally traumatized from the attack was because I'd *forgiven* the man who inflicted it. It was that simple. By forgiving him, I'd set myself free and was then open to receive the lessons and gifts that were offered to me through the experience. If I'd chosen to hold on to fear and anger, if I had continued to tell myself the same frightening, painful story over and over, then that's the energy I would have gone on living with.

Was this incident a terrible thing? For sure. At the time it happened, it was horrifying. But choosing to hold on to that part of the story would be much more damaging. Because my initial reaction early on was to forgive, I was able to let go, grow, and move forward.

Forgiveness does not excuse the other person's actions, and it doesn't mean you have to accept them. It's about setting yourself free from bitterness and taking back your power. It's about letting go of negative energy that's taking up space in your mind where high-quality thoughts should be. It's for you. There's a great quote from the late theologian Lewis B. Smedes that says "To forgive is to set a prisoner free and realize that prisoner was you." This is an absolute truth.

This understanding has led me to change the stories I tell myself about many things that had caused me pain. By looking at each situation and finding empathy, understanding, and forgiveness, I've been able to let go of so much unnecessary junk and open up beautiful, cavernous spaces for good to come into my life. And it has.

There are three great ways to begin the process of forgiving. First, know that the forgiveness is in no way condoning what was done. It has everything to do with you, and really not much at all to do with the other person. It's about letting go of pain and resentment, which is like poison to the spirit. It's about setting yourself free. Think of forgiveness as a spiritual superfood. It's an emotional detox.

Second, understand that whatever the person did, the root cause underneath everything was very likely fear. People so often act out of fear, and when we see this, it can sometimes make a situation a bit easier to digest because acting out of fear is something we all understand. It's about compassion. This also applies when it comes to forgiving yourself.

Finally, shift the way you look at a situation. A change in perception is amazingly freeing. Look for the good, even the smallest molecule, that came out of it: a lesson, an experience, a fire to create a positive change. Right after my experience, I was so thankful that I was alive that just the feeling of gratitude was the first bit of light I was able to see. It helped me open up. Be willing to see the whole thing, all of it, from a different point of view and you'll crack it open so the sun can begin to shine in. This is also a good one when you need to forgive yourself.

After the trial, the young guy in my case was sentenced to nine years in prison. I don't know what happened to him after he got out, but wherever he is, I do hope he has found peace and healing. It may sound crazy, but I send him love. And I hope he has forgiven himself. Forgive, be love, let the light in, and set yourself free. You deserve it.

Day 23
Why You're Exactly Where You Should Be

Sometimes, the place we're in can be a major bummer. Things like losing a job, moving to a new place, or moving on from a

relationship can spin us into a place of wanting to force everything to be okay, right now, when it simply can't. Accepting
what is, turning inward, and giving yourself time to allow
things to flow on their own will empower you to make the right
choices and open your heart and mind up to amazing opportunities that may come your way.

I can remember a time a while back when it felt like so many
things in my life were in transition. While most of it was great
and much needed, change is still not always easy. One of the
most important things I remind myself of when things feel off
track is that it's not necessary to have all the answers right away
and that they'll come when the time is right, every time.

> *"One of the most important things I remind
> myself of when things feel off track is that
> it's not necessary to have all the answers
> right away and that they'll come when
> the time is right, every time."*

When the pressure is off to force answers before they're ready
to appear, and I give myself permission to be exactly where I
am without stressing about tomorrow, it's pretty amazing how
much better I feel. It also helps things unfold exactly as they're
meant to without diversions. I also find myself able to then simply *be in the moment and embrace the journey.*

This isn't to say that it's not important to think things
through and take action when you feel called. It's basically to
say that if you're thinking about things and clear answers aren't
coming to you, then it's perfectly okay to give yourself permission *not* to know. *To tread water for a bit.* Everything becomes
crystal clear in its own time. Sometimes, it just takes a while,
and it may be longer than you'd like it to be.

This is also one of the most important things I find myself reminding clients of when I'm coaching—that knowing *you're exactly where you should be in this moment* and releasing the need to struggle for immediate answers will take the pressure off and help things flow just as they're meant to. It will also keep you more open to new roads that may not have appeared for you if you hadn't stopped to take a breath.

Even positive change can be challenging. Decisions about making a change in your career, moving to a new pad, launching a new project, going back to school . . . all these are great, and at the same time can be pretty overwhelming if we allow them to be. This is also a time to allow answers and guidance to come organically.

During this time, it's also important to be kind to yourself and forgiving of yourself, and to think about treating yourself the same way you would treat a good friend going through the same situation. Know that what got you into this place serves a purpose, even if the purpose hasn't revealed itself yet.

So here's the deal. Give yourself permission to not have all the answers, to take the time you need, and to feel whatever it is you're feeling. Be easy on yourself. Know that everything will happen in its own time, and your job is to make the best of the ride—to turn it into an adventure. This is how you'll land on your feet, every time.

Day 24
Relationships and Life: Here's the Likely Answer When You Feel Like Something's Missing

"Only what you have not given can be lacking in any situation." This is an idea from *A Course in Miracles* that I'm breathing in this week, and have numerous times before. It's a powerful truth that can be challenging to accept because it shows us that we must look at what *we* are not offering in any situation, and that we must take responsibility. Amp up the faith. That in fact, what we give more of is what we will receive more of in return.

For me, this concept is a reminder to always see things from a place of love. It's a reminder to give even more love and to *be* love. This creates big shifts in perception that result in miracles. It also prompts me to turn inward when looking to fill in what's missing in any situation. The answer, and the call to action, is always right there.

This idea is the core place from which to examine any area of our lives that we feel is lacking, especially in relationships. It will always offer the answer we seek when asking how we can improve a situation. In any relationship, if we want more understanding, we must be more understanding. If we want more love, we must give more love and be more loving. If we're looking for more joy and laughter, we must be joy and shine our light to bring laughter to others. And the list goes on.

When I look back on some of my relationships that crashed and burned or endured tremendous challenges, I now see many of those situations so much more clearly. How could I expect someone to give it their all when there were parts of me that I wasn't making available? How could I expect someone to let their walls come down when I myself had concrete walls in place? How could I expect someone to open up to feeling complete love for me when I myself was allowing fear to hold me back from fully expressing my love? I was often frustrated; feeling like another person wasn't open to evolving a relationship when the truth was, it was me who wasn't open. I wasn't *being* what I was seeking.

This is not to say that every single relationship has the potential to be healthy or right. Every relationship, however, is an opportunity to learn and grow. So, in toxic or abusive situations, what's lacking may be the fact that the relationship needs to come to an end but is still ongoing. Therefore, the "what more can I give" becomes the act of letting go. Walking away actually becomes an act of love, as does forgiving and viewing the other person with compassion.

So I invite you to join me in asking this powerful question when facing a challenge or struggle, or when seeking a solution in any situation: "What more can I give?" Then be open to allowing your inner voice to share the honest truth with you. Be willing to take responsibility for that which you're not giving, and then open up to giving freely with all your heart. Being willing to do this has changed so much for me and will continue to do so. It can transform, grow, and even save relationships, and it can definitely create big-time growth within *you*.

> *"Be willing to take responsibility for that which you're not giving, and then open up to giving freely with all your heart."*

Give, take ownership, and shift the way you're viewing the situation. Be willing to go within and then step outside your comfort zone in order to create true, miraculous change. This is where it all begins.

Day 25
Expect Amazing Things—How Expectations Shape Your Days

Much of the way we experience our day comes from what we expect of it. Expect amazing things today and it will be. Expect a bad day and that's pretty much what you'll get. It's pretty simple.

A while back, I took a day off to go stand-up paddleboarding in Malibu. It was totally delicious. The water was gorgeous, the sun was shining, and a pod of dolphins swam by. I'd looked forward to this for days.

I can tell you this for sure the one thing that helped make it so great was that I *expected* it to be! In the days leading up to going, I was making statements (affirmations, really) like "I'm going paddleboarding on Thursday. It's going to be amazing!"

I grew up with a major fear of the ocean. I wouldn't even go in past my knees. For a Southern California girl, you can imagine this might be a bit of an issue. Years ago, I finally set my mind to overcoming the fear, and now I'm passionate about water sports. I snorkel, free dive, surf, and swim. Anywhere in or near the ocean is a very happy place for me! But to be honest, there is still a sneaky little voice inside of me that will creep in and stir up anxiety when I'm faced with going into the open ocean far from the shore.

Before my day off for paddleboarding in Malibu, that annoying little voice was tempting me to make statements like "I'm a little nervous I might fall in" or "Going that far from the shore can be scary." I guarantee if that were the mind-set I'd been in prior to hitting the water, it would have drastically changed my experience. But I chose to ignore those negative, limiting thoughts and instead chose to expect a fantastic experience. And it was.

> *"Changing your outlook and expectations can literally change what you experience."*

Our expectations for the day usually begin in the morning. When you wake up, be conscious about the statements you're making and the thoughts you're choosing about the day ahead. If you're thinking, "That marketing meeting this afternoon is going to suck big time," you're not only setting yourself up for a negative experience, you're also putting out low vibrations that affect other aspects of life, too. Changing your outlook and expectations can literally change what you experience. And aligning your expectations with your positive intentions gives you that much more momentum.

This isn't to say everything will always turn out the way we expect it to. That would be boring! It's also not to say having powerful, positive expectations will never lead to disappointment. That happens sometimes, and there are always lessons to be received there. This is just to say our expectations play a huge role in shaping the way we live—the richness, the light, the growth, and the joy.

So when it comes to creating a fantastic life, be sure to add setting high-quality, positive expectations to your happiness toolbox. It's a powerful thing to expect awesomeness. To expect fantastic experiences. Expect an amazing, delicious, joyful life—and it will be.

Day 26
Why Being a Little Badass Can Be Blissful

I can remember a time when fear about what others would think of me would keep me from expressing my opinion or standing up for myself, even in situations where I should have been putting up a serious fight for what I believed was right. I never had any problem coming out swinging in defense of others, but when I had to defend myself, that was another story. The same fears held me back when it came to busting out of my comfort zone or breaking rules (even the ones that just *ask* to be broken).

A few years ago, I finally drew a line and decided to set free and embrace my inner badass. I must tell you, she's pretty freaking cool. What I've come to know is that when you say what's on your mind, take risks, and express what you desire in a cool, clear, respectful way, you can create powerful change, get more of what you want, and transform potentially negative encounters into positive experiences.

When something doesn't feel right, when you're not being treated with respect and kindness, or when someone does something that you feel is completely out of line, don't be afraid to release your inner badass and tell it like you see it (with grace, of course). You'll be doing yourself a huge favor. And by offering your authentic self and speaking your truth, you're doing a service for others involved as well. The response is often surprisingly positive and empowering.

I've also learned through experience that rocking a bit of moxie when breaking rules or stepping outside of your safe zone can also bring on amazing experiences that may have otherwise been missed. Willingness to take risks and to brave feeling out of your element can spark huge growth and lead to exhilarating experiences you'll never forget.

Until my midtwenties, I was terrified of swimming in the ocean. Then on a trip to Mexico, I was so overwhelmed by the water's beauty that I dedicated myself to breaking free of a lifelong fear and experiencing what it was like to be a part of that amazing beauty. I started slowly, with someone holding on to me as I went in, but it wasn't long before I was swimming like a fish. Releasing that fear opened up an awesome new world. Today, I'm super-passionate about the ocean and its conservation. I've learned to surf, dive, and even swim with sharks (yup . . . in the cage—seriously badass).

"Know that chances for fantastic breakthroughs can sometimes come disguised as uncomfortable situations."

So the next time you're tempted to shy away from speaking what's on your mind or trying something that would usually have you running the other way, rethink the opportunity and the good things that might be waiting for you. Know that chances for fantastic breakthroughs can sometimes come disguised as uncomfortable situations.

The freedom that comes from trying something new, releasing the fear of what others might think, and even breaking the rules now and then is fiercely amazing. When you believe in yourself and treat yourself like the remarkable, capable person you are, you'll put yourself in a place to excel and be of the highest possible service to yourself and to the world. Spread your wings, say it like you mean it, and don't be afraid to shine. You are a badass, and open doors are waiting.

Day 27
Are You Too Hard on Yourself?

So I've been pretty hard on myself lately. I've been letting that get-it-all-done-now voice inside me bug me to no end. I've been putting a lot of pressure on myself to blog more, work on my book more, get more done, juggle more projects, and on it goes. I had to put the brakes on this ridiculousness!

Every now and then, we have to stop and remind ourselves that we are enough, just as we are, we are always doing the best we can, and everything will come together just fine. When we treat ourselves with love and compassion, we are actually *more* productive and can think more clearly than when we are hard on ourselves! Plus, we have a lot more fun!

> "Every now and then, we have to stop and remind ourselves that we are enough, just as we are."

Take a moment right now to breathe in and give yourself credit for how amazing you are. Remind yourself that *you are enough,* that you're doing the best you can. Then do something kind for yourself—even something small that just takes a minute. *Then* you can check back in to your day. Do this regularly (set a reminder in your phone if you feel inspired*). Kindness, compassion, and love for yourself make up a huge part of the foundation for your happiest life.

Day 28
Five Secrets for Successful Business Networking (and Making Friends, Too)

With the huge growth over the last few years of social media platforms and online business networking, the popularity of in-person networking events has also increased, offering infinite opportunities for those who take the initiative to venture out and see what's happening in the world away from the computer screen.

In addition to large networking organizations and general one-size-fits-all networking events, new groups that focus on particular niches or industries are popping up all the time, providing more targeted opportunities for meeting new contacts, mentors, and potential clients. A newer concept in networking circles and events brings trendsetting business leaders and entrepreneurs together with brands, venues, and organizations that are looking to gain exposure with just that crowd, creating a win-win for all.

So how do the savviest networkers make the most of all these opportunities? They follow a few key practices that greatly increase the value of what they take away, as well as what they have to offer others they meet.

Through my years of organizing all kinds of events, working with clients on networking and business building, and, honestly, running into people at networking events who've made me want to run for the hills, I've identified a few practices regularly used by super-successful and dynamic people. Add these to your networking savoir faire, and you'll begin to see big results.

1. Approach each event and the people you meet from the standpoint of "What can I give?" rather than "What can I get?" When you genuinely look to be of service to others, you will be amazed by the doors that will open for you.

2. Don't hand someone your business card within the first two minutes of meeting in an attempt to manufacture a contact without even knowing anything about the person. Random card dropping is generally not productive and can be perceived as disingenuous. More times than not, your card will end up in the circular file. There are rare exceptions to this, so just let your intuition guide you. Instead spend time speaking to those you meet. Find out what they do, where they're from, and even what they like to do outside of business. Be genuinely, enthusiastically interested in people, and quality opportunities, great connections, and even new friendships will come naturally.

3. When someone gives you his or her business card, think of it as a great compliment. Follow the traditional Japanese custom of treating the card, and therefore the person, with great respect. Instead of immediately shoving it in your pocket or handbag, study the card and then hold it with both hands while you continue your conversation. If you spot something on the card that inspires a question or comment, even better. When the time is right, find a quiet way to place the card in a safe spot.

4. Give the person or people you are talking to your full attention. This may sound like a no-brainer, but think of all the people whose eyes are glancing at their phones or darting

around the room to see who else is there while they're half listening to the people they've just met. People pick up on this immediately, and they will remember. It's much more valuable and productive to place your complete focus on the opportunity before you. It's also courteous. If there are other people worth meeting at the same event, you can create that opportunity by finding polite ways to move on when the time is just right. That's the time to be looking for whom you'd like to meet next.

5. Your smile is one of your greatest commodities. It's absolutely 100 percent true, and I can't stress it enough. A warm, authentic smile will open more doors than the shiniest background or business card. Your smile is your greatest chance to make a sparkling impression.

> *"Your smile is your greatest chance to make a sparkling impression."*

Whether you're just starting out in your career, looking to make new friends, launching a new business, or advancing in your profession, effective networking is one of the most important skills you can possess. Learn how to work it in creative, dynamic ways and it will be one of your most valuable keys to greater success in anything you dream to accomplish.

Day 29
Are You Shrinking to Fit? Why the Uncensored You Is Awesome!

I've become very clear on something lately. Much of the damage and frustration that occurs in any relationship or situation in our lives comes from one thing: making ourselves smaller to fit into it.

Playing it small and safe in life and in relationships can be like a low-grade fever or a slow-moving infection. You don't realize it's happening until you actually go for a checkup and discover it's there. You've been puttering along just fine as is. But the damage is happening, and something must be done before it gets serious.

> *"Playing it small and safe in life and in relationships can be like a low-grade fever or a slow-moving infection. You don't realize it's happening until you actually go for a checkup and discover it's there."*

If you're holding back and dimming your light out of fear that you may be too bold, say or do the wrong thing, be rejected, or rock the boat, you're shrinking yourself and your life, as well as denying the world—and yourself—your true, amazing gifts.

I can remember a past relationship where I totally did this. I would bite my tongue to avoid conflict, turn down opportunities that I thought he wouldn't approve of, and worst of all, avoid taking risks and chances in my business because of fear that if I failed, I would disappoint him. And none of this had anything to do with him. It was all my doing. In fact, it was so unfair to him because the person he wanted to be with was *me*. Not a smaller version of me. Not the PG-rated version of me. He didn't want the "lite" version of me; he wanted the *light* version of me!

So here's the deal. You are good enough. You're amazing, in fact. Your thoughts and dreams are valid and powerful. Express and pursue them daringly. The greatest change-makers are the ones who aren't afraid to ruffle a few feathers along their paths. *What you're capable of if you free yourself to be the complete, uncensored you may blow your mind.* This is also the path to your happiest, most peaceful self.

Forget the critics. Let go of the fear of screwing up—know that it's part of making great things happen. Be willing to step out of your own way and take chances. Trust that the universe is there to support you.

The world and the people in your life are in great need of your light. You, in all your YOUness, are exactly why people will want to work with you, be in relationships with you, and support you. If you begin to play small, purposely downplay your dreams and desires, and label yourself as "shrink to fit," you're not doing them—or yourself—any favors.

I believe what we all need to do is train ourselves to regularly check in with our inner voices to be sure we're being true to our whole selves and what we really, truly, deeply desire. Shrinking ourselves to fit into different situations can be a defense habit that comes to us automatically and can be a tough one to recognize and take charge of. It sure was for me. What I finally realized was that I was more concerned about the approval of others than I was about achieving my own dreams and desires.

The good news is that just like shifting any habit or pattern, by becoming conscious of the tendency to fall into the shrinking state of being, we can change the direction of our sails and head back to where the sun is shining.

Creating this shift may mean some of the people and situations in our lives that are not in alignment with our best lives and highest purposes fall away, which can be very hard at times. The key is to fully trust what's truly meant for you will remain, and that space will be created for the awesome.

By fully committing yourself to be your brightest, follow your dreams, and be your authentic, passionate self in every area of your life, you'll naturally attract the relationships and opportunities that will lift you up, back you up, and empower you. Awesome doors will begin to fly open and invite you in. Life will flow with much more ease and clarity. This is the cycle of an authentic, powerful, joyful life.

Where in your life are you shrinking to fit? Playing small? Containing your voice? It's time to set your full, beautiful, dynamic self completely and totally free. Your soul and the world will be grateful.

Day 30
Three Ways to Be Happier Now

I really love my life! It wasn't always that way. It took a lot of hard work, important lessons, and many shifts in perception to get to this place. I've learned to step into myself and who I truly am, and I've learned to get out of my own way.

Something else I learned along the way is that all human beings have a single life purpose in common. That purpose is to be happy. For a big part of my life, I spent so much time struggling, trying to figure out how to feel happier, to get to a happier place, or to get my hands around the next thing or achievement that would "make me happy." It never seemed to work. I know now that what I didn't do was just allow myself to simply be happy right then and there.

The truth is that authentic happiness and inner peace lies in the present moment, right now, within us, waiting and longing to be embraced. Once I finally understood this idea, my life changed profoundly.

Along my own journey to be happy, I discovered a number of ideas and tools to assist in embracing the joy that is always available in each moment. There are three, in particular, I've found to be fantastically helpful.

First, view happiness as a skill and as an activity and not just as a feeling but also as something we take active part in doing and creating. Aristotle said "Happiness is a state of activity." This notion entirely changed my perception. When we're in the midst of actively doing something we enjoy, being of service to others, or taking part in something healthful like exercise, meditation, or munching down a big salad, we feel happy and empowered. This is doing happiness. It's all about choosing how we create and live each moment.

Second, rethink mornings. Our thoughts have a deep impact on our world. I remember a time when I was waking up each day in a place of complete lack, swimming in negative, limiting thoughts that left me forcing myself to get out of bed with a heavy heart on a regular basis. Skipping breakfast, loading up on caffeine, and rushing to get out the door on time didn't help. I was carrying that nasty energy with me into the day ahead.

Once I realized that the way I was starting my day was creating the path for the rest of it, I understood how extremely important it is to make mornings as positive as possible. I've now changed my thoughts in the mornings to focus on the positive, and I've changed my routine to include plenty of time, a decent breakfast, and reading uplifting posts from my favorite blogs. It's worked wonders. My days, and my life, have radically improved.

Finally, open yourself to recognize and receive the limitless joy, comfort, and wonder that is all around at every moment in the little things. This is excellent everyday practice, but it's especially helpful during challenging times. It's easy to get so caught up in focusing on the big stuff in life we miss the bliss that can be found in all the amazing, beautiful small things, which actually aren't small at all.

The orchid plant in my office is a great example. Sometimes, when I'm feeling a bit stressed, I focus on the remarkable intricacy and beauty of this living miracle, and it really puts things in perspective. I also have a super-cute glass flying pig on my desk to remind me to say "no" when I need to. It makes me smile every time I look at it and serves as a great reminder to be true to myself. That little winged pig has a big impact.

> *"Your happiest place is right here, right now—in this moment. Live it. Rock it."*

Changing the way we perceive happiness can completely transform the way we experience it, as well as greatly increase its presence. I believe the same applies to balance, love, and passion. It's all about choice, thoughts, and taking an active role in doing, creating, recognizing, and embracing. Your happiest place is right here, right now—in this moment. Live it. Rock it. Make it beautiful.

SUGGESTED READING

For worksheets, bonus downloads, and more resources for *Operation Happiness*, visit kristiling.com/operationhappinessresources.

ONLINE

More from Kristi:

kristiling.com

More Information and Resources on Ho'oponopono:

hooponopono.org

hooponoponoway.net

zero-wise.com

Resources for Daily Positive Reading:

rodalewellness.com

aspiremag.net

success.com

tinybuddha.com

simplereminders.com

RECOMMENDED BOOKS

On Happiness, Love, and Spiritual Growth:

The Easiest Way to Live: Let Go of the Past, Live in the Present, and Change Your Life Forever by Mabel Katz

A Return to Love: Reflections on the Principles of a Course in Miracles by Marianne Williamson

Wabi Sabi Love: The Ancient Art of Finding Perfect Love in Imperfect Relationships by Arielle Ford

The Four Agreements: A Practical Guide to Personal Freedom by Don Miguel Ruiz

The Power of Intention: Learning to Co-Create Your World Your Way by Dr. Wayne W. Dyer

Happy for No Reason: 7 Steps to Being Happy from the Inside Out by Marci Shimoff

Before Happiness: The 5 Hidden Keys to Achieving Success, Spreading Happiness, and Sustaining Positive Change by Shawn Achor

Easy Breezy Prosperity: The 5 Foundations for a More Joyful, Abundant Life by Emmanuel Dagher

On Loss, Grief, and Transition:

Second Firsts: Live, Laugh, and Love Again by Christina Rasmussen

Broken Open: How Difficult Times Can Help Us Grow by Elizabeth Lesser

On Diet and Wellness:

Crazy Sexy Kitchen: 150 Plant-Empowered Recipes to Ignite a Mouthwatering Revolution by Kris Carr

The Happiness Diet: A Nutritional Prescription for a Sharp Brain, Balanced Mood, and Lean, Energized Body by Tyler G. Graham and Drew Ramsey

The Single Source Cancer Course: The Layperson's Guide to Preventing, Treating, and Surviving Cancer—Volume 1: Prevention by S. Wilking Horan

INDEX

Underscored page references indicate sidebars.

1141

$\frac{1}{5}\frac{4}{6}\frac{3}{7}$